"I used these ideas in class and had a wonderful day with my students."

Thank you so much!! I used these ideas in class and had a wonderful day with my students. As a first Year Relief Teacher I find this site invaluable in helping me become a better and more confident Teacher.

Jess (Take Control of the Noisy Class customer)

*   *   *

"It is very rewarding to see a teacher apply strategies from Rob's materials, then get excited as they see the 'magic' work."

"The materials have been right on target, students have benefitted as well as teachers. It is very rewarding to see a teacher apply strategies from Rob's materials, then get excited as they see the 'magic' work. Thank you for making my job easier and validating the experience."

Cheryl E. Le Fon (Take Control of the Noisy Class customer)

The Behaviour Toolkit

Behaviour Solutions for Today's Tough Classrooms

THE ULTIMATE collection of ANSWERS to your most frustrating classroom management problems & questions

Rob Plevin

http://www.needsfocusedteaching.com

About the Author

Rob Plevin is an ex-deputy head teacher and Special Education Teacher with the practical experience to help teachers in today's toughest classrooms.

No stranger to behaviour management issues, Rob was 'asked to leave' school as a teenager. Despite his rocky route through the education system he managed to follow his dream of becoming a teacher after spending several years working as an outdoor instructor, corporate trainer and youth worker for young people in crisis. Since then he has worked with challenging young people in residential settings, care units and tough schools and was most recently employed as Deputy Head at a PRU for children and teenagers with behaviour problems. He was identified as a key player in the team which turned the unit round from 'Special Measures'.

He now runs needsfocusedteaching.com, is the author of several books and presents training courses internationally for teachers, lecturers, parents and care workers on behaviour management & motivation. His live courses are frequently described as 'unforgettable' and he was rated as an 'outstanding' teacher by the UK's Office for Standards in Education.

Rob's courses and resources feature the Needs-Focused Approach™ – a very effective system for preventing and dealing with behaviour problems in which positive staff/student relationships are given highest priority.

To book Rob for INSET or to enquire about live training please visit the help desk at

www.needsfocusedteaching.com

Introduction

Welcome!

The Behaviour Toolkit is a handy reference tool for busy teachers like you. It's a collection of proven positive techniques and strategies you can use in response to the frustrating student behaviour problems you're likely to encounter in today's classrooms.

The first section of the book consists of comprehensive answers to questions most frequently asked by teachers dealing with specific troublesome student behaviours. The answers are presented and explained as step-by-step strategies, with a variety of solutions for each problem being offered. In most cases the answers explain exactly what to do in response to the behaviour as well as what to avoid doing so that you don't inadvertently cause the situation to escalate.

In addition, whenever you see this...

[Questions from the Real World]

...you'll find answers from top trainers and behaviour consultants given in response to questions raised during some of our online Q & A sessions and live interviews.

The second section consists of 'Quick Strategies' which you can use as handy reminders for most of the behaviour problems you're likely to experience in the classroom. There's no padding with this section – it's basically just a straightforward list of responses which you can quickly look up and try.

I sincerely hope you find the answers you're looking for in the Behaviour Tool Kit but I have to add a word of caution before you dive in. The strategies, while effective in their own right, work best when used as part of what I call the **Needs Focused ApproachTM.**

In essence, this is basically a way of communicating and dealing with students within a positive framework of respectful, positive relationships but when used consistently, it can bring about rapid and quite dramatic improvements in any classroom.

You can read all about the Needs Focused ApproachTM in the Classroom Management Mini-Course which accompanies this resource. Just sign up below and we'll send it to you in bite-sized chunks via email...

Get your FREE Classroom Management Mini-Course and Learn the Step-by-Step System That Reduces 90% of all Classroom Discipline Problems in Record Time

Sign up for your FREE copy here:

http://needsfocusedteaching.com/kindle/behaviour/

OK, that's it for the introduction – let's get straight to the strategies...

Motivation/work-related problems

Dealing with students who don't bring equipment to class

This is one of those seemingly unimportant management issues which is often swept under the carpet by a teacher who is frantically trying to concentrate efforts on more serious issues. In a lively class, when you've got Mary and Matilda cat fighting, Liam smoking, Carl spitting on Graham, Steven chucking text books at Johnny and Paul making lewd comments about the support assistant's chest – all at the same time – it's easy just to hand a spare pen to Kyle who's forgotten his. After all, there's no need to get in a lather over the small stuff. Is there?

One reason we should be at least a little concerned about Kyle's missing pen is that seemingly trivial things like this can easily trip up the most well-prepared classroom manager if they get out of hand. Why?

Because whatever you allow to happen in class, you effectively encourage.

Every time you hand over a pen from your dwindling pile of spares you effectively train your little angels in the belief that it's perfectly acceptable to come to class without one. So before long, they're all at it. Suddenly, one pen becomes thirty five, you spend half the lesson handing pens out like sweeties and you're left with a handful of chewed gunky biros and a group of kids who couldn't give two hoots about coming to class prepared!

The bottom line is that you want to minimise the number of excuses that students will have for not starting work. Let's face it, not having a pen is a great excuse to avoid transferring words on to paper; not having a ruler is a great excuse to avoid measuring or drawing straight lines; not having coloured pens means you can't finish your illustrations, and not having a drawing compass makes it absolutely impossible to draw circles and give the student in front of you impromptu body piercings.

The more time you spend sourcing, fetching, carrying and monitoring equipment and resources (you do keep a record of items you lend out don't you?) the more stressful your lessons will be, the less time you'll have to support and manage your students, and the more dependent they will become. That's before we take into account valuable text books and exercise books which are taken home and never seen again. Let's get on top of this issue and make life easier for everyone.

Here are eight classroom management strategies for dealing with it...

1. Text books and exercise books – keep them in your room. I'm sure there is some complex mathematical formula to explain the relationship between a student's general classroom behaviour and the likelihood that he or she will return a book once it has been taken home - but let's just say that with a challenging group it's not very likely at all. And it causes huge problems.

I remember being pretty lax when it came to taking my own exercise books home as a student – they just seemed to disappear once they entered the depths of my school bag, never to be seen again. I had a new exercise book in some lessons almost every week – so by the end of term there were hundreds of little books with 'Robert Plevin' labels on them lying round in uncharted places, each containing about three pages of work. Maybe it's just (disorganised) boys but it's a problem which needs solving if you, as a teacher, don't want all your lessons turned upside down with cries of "Miss, I need a new book".

Your best bet is not to let them take them home in the first place. Store exercise books on a dedicated class shelf. Yes, I know you have to set homework but there's nothing wrong with giving them a separate homework folder/book/file specifically for homework. And never send text books home – that's what photocopiers are for.

2. Pens and other equipment - Offer to lend them some of your equipment in return for 'collateral' such as a shoe. Like all the strategies in this resource, there are going to be some which you don't feel comfortable about using. This is probably one of them purely because it can get very smelly in a hot classroom when half the students are minus their full complement of footwear.

Having said that, it is a very effective way of making sure you get your equipment back at the end of the lesson. Though now I come to think of it, I do still have a large collection of odd Woolworths plastic trainers; for some reason they seemed to think a new HB pencil was a fair swap.

3. Encourage them to borrow from each other. This is preferable to having to continually give out materials from your own stocks. Give a brief period of time at the start of the lesson for students to borrow items from other members of the class. Be prepared to change strategy if they start removing each other's shoes.

4. Use a more positive approach. With any classroom problem there are two ways of approaching it – reward positive behaviour or punish inappropriate behaviour. Rather than focusing on students who don't bring equipment, it might be better to reward those who do with spontaneous light-hearted treats (such as a garishly decorated plastic pen or antique Woolworths training shoe).

5. Focus on teaching the behaviour you want to see. This is my personal favourite. I'm a big fan of methods which develop independence – give a man a fish and all that – and the more you can lead your students towards becoming responsible, the easier (and more meaningful) your job will be. Give them a checklist to take home and fill in every morning with items they should bring to school. Then show them how to use the checklist as a memory aid – "have a quick look through it in a morning and check off items as you add them to your bag."

6. Get the parents/carers involved. Inform parents that this key issue is causing great concern - explain how it is impacting on the child's progress in other lessons and its importance as a life/employment skill. You could also mention that unorganised teenagers tend to lack the ability to move out of the parental home and often end up living their well into their thirties. That usually gets them listening. Show them the checklist you've created and ask them to remind the student each morning/evening to use it.

7. Be prepared. Always have a complete box of materials and equipment on your desk – your 'Resource Box'. Cut out the tendency for students to keep/borrow/forget to give back/steal your materials by having them clearly and boldly marked. Pink nail varnish tends to be a good deterrent if you're lending materials to boys.

8. Keep a clear record. A great way to impress students with the impact of their actions is to give them a clear picture of how significant a particular problem is. A chart provides a clear record, for both teacher and student, of how many times materials have been forgotten. It also gives a definite starting point from which to improve:

"Nathan, you have forgotten your materials every day this week, let's see if we can get one positive mark on the chart tomorrow shall we?"

Dealing with inappropriate comments from students

There are always going to be students who try to make us feel uncomfortable by asking increasingly personal, inappropriate, silly questions. This is especially common when we get a new class to teach – whether it's the start of term or a cover lesson and it is a scenario which must be dealt with swiftly – otherwise your control over the class can be severely eroded.

"Why are you late Sir?"

"Were you out last night Sir?"

"Where did you go Sir?"

"Do you drink Sir?"

"Were you drinking last night Sir?"

"Is that why you're late Sir?"

"Did you pull Sir?"

"Does your wife know Sir?"

"Have you got a wife Sir?"

"Is she nice looking Sir?"

...and so on.

They do this to gain attention, hold up lessons and look good in front of their friends; to try and find our weaknesses, to embarrass us and ultimately wind us up. Sometimes they try to shock us in front of their peers as a way of displaying or increasing their status and sometimes they just want to have a laugh. Other times it may be because they feel they have known us long enough to warrant being over-familiar.

Such situations, harmless as they may first seem, need to be cut early before they get out of hand. If you go along with the first few questions more and more students will get drawn in, and once that happens the comments get worse; becoming sillier, ruder and more personal until the situation becomes very difficult to control.

The result is, at best, a very annoyed and embarrassed member of staff, a loss of respect, damaged relationships and a class of very excited students – some of whom are likely to be given sanctions they will consider unfair and that could have been avoided.

One way to deal with this type of questioning is to take the attention away from the child as soon as possible. The following techniques are excellent for doing that and should be used whenever you are faced with inappropriate questions or insults from a student:

1) Calmly state that the conversation is inappropriate and must stop:

"That comment is inappropriate/unacceptable. You need to think before saying things like that."

"We'll talk about these comments later."

Make the statement without emotion and then move on with the lesson. It should be a complete brush off. Don't get drawn into a conversation with this person and don't answer any more of their comments – you've dealt with them and they deserve no more of your attention.

2) Create a diversion such as a quick demonstration, introducing a new topic/game etc.

"Look this way everyone please, I set this up earlier."

"OK, for this game you need a blue pen and a piece of scrap paper..."

Once again, the secret is to move on from their questions straight away and change the focus of attention. In order to be able to do this on your toes and not get caught out trying to think of suitable alternative activities you really should have a resource file (either in your head or hard copy) of interesting and engaging games and fill-in activities.

3) Take out a pen and paper and say:

"I'm writing your comments down; I'm recording what you say so that I don't make a mistake when I explain your behaviour to other people."

4) Use Humour:

While you should avoid hitting out with sarcasm and personal slights, stealing the attention with correct use of humour can be a nice way of diverting attention.

"Do you believe in freedom, because if you keep making comments like that you're going to lose yours at break-time."

"Three simple instructions ... Shut Up, Sit Down and Hold your breath until you are a uniform shade of red."

Dealing with students who have no interest in the lesson

A student who has no interest in lessons and anything you say and do can have a terrible impact on the rest of the class. What you must remember however is that this student probably wants to succeed – most do, at heart - but has virtually given up due to a succession of failures, discouragement and low self-image. It may take time to reach this student and help him see life (including your lessons) differently but there are definitely steps to take which will help turn the situation round more quickly.

1. Look to sincerely praise anything and everything you can. Students with a very low self-image may be uncomfortable receiving praise in front of others so begin by using written praise. Send notes home, leave post-it notes or written comments in their books, send them cards or typed letters on school-headed paper stating how pleased you are with their efforts, and include anything positive you have heard from another teacher. This young person needs to know he has potential and that somebody is taking the time to notice. Sincere praise is one of the most powerful tools you possess and as long as he understands that you actually do want to help him – and not just 'get him to listen because it's your job' - this student will respond.

2. Do some research. Speak to other teachers, their form tutor or head of year to find out if there are any underlying issues you should be aware of. A tutor who has a good relationship with a particularly hard to reach student can give you 'insider tips' to connect with this student as well as notify you of any issues to avoid.

3. Schedule a '1 to 1' meeting with the student. Purpose: to ask why they are so uninterested, ask their advice on making lessons more engaging for them and help them to see the relevance of what they are being asked to do.

If you feel they are unlikely to turn up for a 1:1 meeting, don't worry - you can increase the chances by proposing it at the right time. There's no point telling them you want to see them in your office when they're in their 'I hate you and your lessons' mood; they won't be interested. Wait, instead, for a time when they are going to be more receptive. A good time is when they've done something well, when you've praised them for a job well done, when you've just complimented them on their work, or a new pair of shoes, or a haircut, or creative use of smiling muscles – i.e. when they are more receptive.

For example, if they play football on the school team, try and find the time to go and watch the game. They'll see you on the side line and will appreciate it. Next time you see them you can mention the game and talk about the goal they scored or their part in the brilliant teamwork. Now they're listening, they know you have interest in them and they know that you want to help them. This would be a better time to suggest the meeting.

4. Change seating. Put them with a partner or other group members who will encourage them and help them.

5. Put them in a mixed ability learning team of 3-4 and give them a definite role or responsibility. Assign them a role that plays to their strengths or abilities. For example if they are good at drawing let them be in charge of graphics or illustrations. If they have trouble sitting still let them be a 'runner' in charge of collating materials, equipment and resources.

6. Involve parents/carers. Having parents on board is a big advantage dealing with any student problems – the more we can present a united front between school and home, the better. The problem, as we all know, is that some parents just don't seem interested – or the student doesn't think they are.

It's a huge problem when parents and other family members have deeply entrenched, negative experiences of school going back through several generations; they'll be hesitant in dealings with teachers. If they themselves failed at school and consequently aren't living the life of their dreams, it's not surprising that they lack the faith in education we expect and need them to have. If in addition their child has been a source of constant distress at school, any contact the parents have had with staff at the school is likely to have been negative. They'll have been told when he has been missing school, when he's repeatedly failed to hand in homework, when he's been in a fight and when he's been abusive to a member of staff.

They won't have heard a word when he's done something well. A good way, if not the only way, to start to get these parents on side is to change their expectation that every communication from school will be a negative one. The more time you spend connecting with them through regular positive contact, the more they will get used to the idea that a call from school doesn't automatically ruin their day.

A 30-second update a couple of times a week – "Hi Maureen, just a quickie to let you know he's been great this week; homework was in on time and he managed to keep it together in maths again." – goes a long way towards doing this. And despite what anyone says, I've witnessed enough 'hard' fathers and 'rough' mothers breaking down in tears in my office when given news of a son or daughter's good progress to believe that this is worth doing.

For a complete resource kit on harnessing support from parents see one of our titles - 'Get The Parents On Board'.

7. Give them a taste of success. Students who are reluctant to take part probably see no value in learning because they never feel they've learned anything. Here's a practical way to give them a sense of accomplishment and leave your lesson feeling they've actually had some success. When they leave feeling like that, they will return in a more positive frame of mind...

i) Ask them a question at the start of the lesson related to the lesson content. They will probably refuse to answer but that's okay – it's probably their fear of looking 'too clever' or fear of making a fool of themselves.

ii) Take the pressure off them by offering them to nominate a friend who can help them answer the question/answer it for them. This is easy for them to do – but the key is that they will see themselves as being involved in the answering process.

iii) Ask them to paraphrase what their friend said so that they answer the question themselves.

iv) Later in the lesson, when other students are involved in independent study, coach the student further by getting them to answer the question for you again on a 1:1 basis. Encourage them to break the answer down into clear steps so that they are totally sure of the process. Offer a little extra 'in-depth' information to add to their answer and ask them once more to show off their new knowledge and tell you 'all they know' about the subject. Congratulate them and tell them you will be asking them at the end of the lesson to repeat their answer to help the other students remember (the extra 'in-depth' knowledge you've given them will give them the opportunity to shine if they wish).

v) At the end of the lesson let them leave on a high by answering the question again as part of your plenary session.

vi) Get them to answer the question next lesson as part of your starter.

Remember that you don't need to limit this strategy to just one student during a lesson. You can feasibly have four or five students all leaving class feeling that they've actually learned something.

8. Use Questions to Grab Your Students' Attention and Get Them Involved

Before I present a near fool-proof way of getting a challenging group of students involved at the start of the lesson let's look at something you should try to avoid: asking the wrong type of questions. It's the most effective way to lose their interest.

Many teachers will start a lesson with a question relating to the topic focus. For example, in a lesson on the circulatory system, the opening question might be: *"How many of you can explain what a blood vessel is?"*

Questions like this may generate some participation but for every hand that goes up there will be ten more that don't. Most of the students, particularly in a low ability or challenging group, will simply ignore this question because it demands something they don't like to (or cannot) display – evidence of prior knowledge about the subject. Let's face it, in a challenging group it's not always cool to know the answers.

A reliable way to get more of your students involved at the start of the lesson – particularly the non-volunteers who don't seem to want to learn - is simply to change the type of questions you ask them.

Let's return to the circulatory system to illustrate what I mean. The average challenging student doesn't even care what a blood vessel is, so asking them about it will be in vain. If we're going to grab their attention we need to ask them something they can relate to. See if you can spot the best question in the following sets:

A) Who can tell me how blood gets round the body?

B) Who knows what a blood vessel is?

C) Can anyone tell me what a blood capillary is?

D) Have you ever cut yourself?

Or:

A) Give me five differences between Macbeth's character before and after he kills Duncan.

B) How does Macbeth change after he kills Duncan?

C) What words would you use to describe Macbeth at the start of the play?

D) When was the last time you did something really terrible that you later regretted?

Can you see why a group of disengaged students would be most likely to respond to 'D' in both cases? Those questions hook them in by giving them opportunity to think about events that are relevant to them or have had a direct effect on them. They appeal to the students because they present an opportunity to share their experiences.

Once you have them hooked, once they are animated and actively taking part – by now no doubt sharing tales of bleeding limbs - then you can lead them into the lesson content. From there, going back to our lesson on circulation, we could go on to ask:

How long did it bleed for?

How did you stop the bleeding?

Do you think it would it have stopped if you had just left it?

And then finally, to lead the students in to the main content of the lesson:

Where does the blood come from and how does it get to the cut?

...and in this way we adapt our questions and make them more relevant to our students so that we get their attention.

Students who say they are bored

[Questions from the Real World]

Andy Vass

Question: How can I keep my confidence when a student causes problems in a lesson just because the subject matter is easy for him/her or they want to spend their time in a more interesting way?

Andy Vass: Again without sounding flippant, make it more interesting. It really isn't about the teacher's level of confidence here; it's about the curriculum challenge. It kind of becomes 2 issues. First and foremost – differentiate – make sure that the student is challenged. High challenge = low stress.

It comes back down to 2 things – finding more challenging/stimulating materials and asking the student what would help him/her. Have a discussion about it – they will often tell you what they need to be engaged, because they are the ones that know most. Talk to colleagues and see how they handle the situation. If you are in a high school and the other teachers teach that student – how do they find him/her? What do they do that works? Share those kinds of things. Use the child as a mentor to others, use their expertise, challenge and stretch them – but remember it's only a short term process otherwise they just end up helping others not growing themselves and that is not useful.

I will throw in a couple of ideas that I recommend you should have a look at. They are great books I wish I had read before I started teaching, they are fantastic. The first is a very practical book called, "The Lazy Teacher's Handbook" by Jim Smith. Lazy Teacher is not a lazy teacher it is somebody who gets the kids working much harder than they do. The paradox is that the lazy teachers work really, really hard to help make sure that the kids work harder than them. The other one is "Young, Gifted and Bored" by David George. David is one of the world's leaders around gifted education and challenging and stretching kids.

So that is the first thing that I would do and that has definitely got to be in this sequence. Second, when all this is in place then you have to maintain what is called a class discipline plan. The students are working to their potential and they are being stretched, if they still chose to disrupt then that is not to do with the curriculum materials, that is to do with the behavioural situation and we handle that in the same way as we would any other student.

[Questions from the Real World]

Julia Thompson & Rob Plevin

Question: How can I motivate passive students? How about those in their final year at school and given up due to poor expectations? What about those who fail in a subject which they perceive to have no value to them?

Julia Thompson: You know this is heartbreaking and it is becoming a global problem. I am going to be honest – I am not going to say 'if you do this and that your strategy will help' because it won't necessarily. You may not be able to turnaround a child – particularly an older child. If a student is in his final year of school all you can do is strengthen them and give them everything you can. Try 2 or 3 different motivational strategies every day.

Treat them with as much dignity as you can. Pay attention and listen to them, be honest with them. And they will need a goal, set a goal for your students and do everything you can to help them. The last thing I would say here is I have just been in with somebody who has been out of school and try to get that person to help.

Rob Plevin: I think this is an area that breaks many teachers – they give, give and give because they want the best for these kids but they see little, if any, improvement. It's so sad. I have seen teachers giving up their jobs because they have been unable to help kids turn round. It's the same for some of the parents, perhaps even worse actually because even though they do everything they can to help, the parents are the last person or people they will listen to.

You will always find that these kids will trust a member of staff much more than a member of the family so we are in a very privileged position that we can actually help these children. But it's got to start with the relationship and if you are the one that can give that kid that extra hand up, a shoulder to cry on, a non-judgemental ear to talk to etc. you have a good chance of bonding with them. When they are in an emotional state –very sad, very fed up, whatever, it can be a very good time to connect with them, to be the person they need. Relationships are built, to some extent, by showing the other person that we care about them – so when students are at their most fragile and emotional, it's actually an opportunity to show we are there for them.

Younger students who have no interest in the lesson

[Questions from the Real World]

Angela Watson & Rob Plevin

Question: How can I hold the interest of the smaller children for more than 30 minutes?

Angela: This is what I talk about in the book as well as the webinar series and that is something I created. Research tells us that small children's attention spans are very short. As a classroom teacher you see that for yourself, you don't need an expert to tell you that. So you realise that if you are trying to get kids to attend to the same task or focusing for 30 minutes or more, it's usually going to be a very frustrating experience so break it up as much as you can, try not to have kids do the same activity for more than 15 minutes. Maybe you can do something like a 10 minute mini-lesson, 20 minutes apart from your work and then come back together as a whole class again for the last 10 minutes. Instead of just 30 minutes with you talking and the kids paying attention to you.

The less whole class teacher directed instruction you do the better your students are going to listen. You have to move away from that model of 'teacher stands in front of the room and talks and the kids have to follow along', it's very difficult for students so try to have them actively involved. You can get individual white boards and have them write their answer on their board and have them hold it up so you can see. You can have them show the answers on their hands, there are all kind of different things you can do to actively involved and minimizing the time when they are sitting and listening to you passively.

Rob: Great answer. I will just add to that if I may. One thing I was fixated with when I started teaching was putting fun in lessons. I had spent a few years in corporate entertainment and I used to put crazy activities in all my lessons to get the kids laughing but it became a situation where I was more the 'entertainer' and they were just the audience that sat there and watched. It was great for a few lessons - we had a laugh and they really enjoyed me being silly but it wasn't really getting them engaged in a lesson and I think you have really hit on the key point there, it's about getting active participation more than entertainment. So one key is to make sure that you have an activity which is set at the right level of challenge; something they can do which is not too easy and not too hard - it's just right. A bit like the porridge in the story of the Three Bears.

Students who won't/ can't work independently

[Questions from the Real World]

Julia Thompson & Rob Plevin

Question: How do I get students to become more independent and less dependent on me? Their parents do everything for them at home - they have no responsibilities so when I have them try to work independently they are unable to do so.

Julia Thompson: One of my things that I found out was, what kind of jobs do they do at home? And if they say, oh I don't have any job at home, I say, oh my gosh because I know that is going to be a struggle. So first of all you need to know (now this is relevant to all grades, this is not just a little kid problem or day care problem, it is for everybody), now when I have students like this I start slowly, one step at a time – using some of the strategies we talked about just like question no. 8 – give them choices, keep them going, make them feel successful, say "this is what you are going to do – I expect you to do it."

Also I give students tasks in my classroom not necessarily just learning tasks but when they are in the classroom they are busy you know – put this up on the board, who's on the board this week? Who's got the class log for when people are absent this week? – I keep them busy. I do not want them to feel helpless – "do you know how to do it? Get your friend to help, but it's got to be done today."

One thing I do is to let them help each other, if they can help someone else, if they can help a younger kid that would be really cool if they could do that. I also like to make sure that their work is short and manageable so it's not overwhelming – you know you can do these five problems. I like to put up a graph and say, "look let's graph this out - you've got this check done, you've done this, this and this - you are on your way."

Rob Plevin: You mentioned about getting them to help other people, that's a brilliant idea, the support programme is just so good and that kind of links back to what I was saying about those girls being put into homes and centres where they were working with people less fortunate than themselves applying that to the classroom is getting kids to help each other and it's surprising how much that helps. On this particular question the only thing I was going to add was starting small and again giving them small chunks - and of course, making sure to praise them when they do something right.

Set them a target of working for five minutes independently and then "you are achieving something that you haven't managed to do before, certainly not for a long time" - acknowledge their improvements. I am going to answer a question that came in on the chat desk which said, "After you have given them a target what will you do if they still won't do the work?" I would just like to add to that that is when you need to have consequence solutions put in place because we can bend over backwards doing all the supportive stuff and doing the relationship stuff and do everything we can to encourage them but eventually there has to be this hard line boundary that kicks in and so if you haven't done your work even when I gave you the five minutes target, you must now face the consequences.

The use of consequences is quite a in-depth subject and I am not going to go into it here - we do it in various different ways on the behaviour needs website (there is a free video on consequences on our blog, actually) but basically you MUST have those stepped consequences in place.

[Questions from the Real World]

Angela Watson

Question: How do I deal with children who are easily distracted and constantly need to be reminded what to do?

Angela: First and foremost I would say, "Don't drive yourself crazy with this". You can't force a child to pay attention, you can't make them be on task, you can put the supports in place to help them but if you focus all of your energy and attention on that child who is daydreaming you are just going to go crazy, and if they are not distracting other kids there is even less of a reason to get worked up about it.

Don't let it drive you crazy, focus on what is going right in the classroom, the children who are ready to learn. When you have a moment walk over to that child tap their paper to refocus them – if everybody else has put their name on their paper and they are just sitting there – just tap the paper and then they will notice they haven't put their name on, just roll your eyes and walk away, you don't have to say a word. You can also find them a buddy. Pick a child who naturally is a little bit bossy, who likes to tell other people what to do and channel that energy into a constructive way, and teaching that child how to be helpful, how to be supportive, how to be constructive and then you are kind of killing two birds with one stone.

In an extreme situation where the child is constantly off task or needs constant reminders about what to do, put five counters or tokens on the child's desk and have a conversation with them and say, "Now I have to tell you what to do a lot of times during the day and it's hard for me because I need to be focussing on teaching the class and I want you to be really in charge of paying attention for yourself so here's what I am going to do to help you. Each time I have to remind you what to do I am going to walk over and take one of these counters and take it from your desk and put it on my desk and you don't even have to attach a consequence to it. You could if you think what's best for the child, just that act of moving the counter off the desk makes them aware of how many times they're not paying attention.

I have done this and I was absolutely amazed at how well it works especially with one particular child. It was probably the most extreme situation that I have ever had. I had to re-focus him probably about 10 times an hour and once I tried this I never had to take away more than those 5 tokens in an entire day. So we went from probably 30 times a day in looking at him and try to re-focus him, to less than 5 times per day, I would just walk over to his desk, take a token from his desk and put it on mine. He guarded those tokens like they were his prized possession! If you put the responsibility on the child and they monitor their own behaviour and do it in a concrete and tangible way like that, it can really help them to be aware, because a lot of those kids just don't realise they are daydreaming and they don't realise how many reminders they need. So something like that can just make it a little bit more obvious for them.

Learned helplessness – dealing with students who give up too easily

[Questions from the Real World]

Julia Thompson & Rob Plevin

Question: We have a kid who just gives up when he is faced with any independent work, he puts his head on the desk and just says he can't do it even when it has been differentiated. How do I deal with this 'Learned Helplessness'?

Julia: I have a million different ways of handling this but I have a couple of things that I have felt most successful. I don't spend a lot of time with a child who is has a sense of helplessness and is feeling pitiful, who is trying to get control and attention from me with the − "oh my God I can't do this, this is too hard." I go to the desk and I say "here's your work, I know you can do this", and, business-like I put the work down, "you need to do this, I will show you how to do it." And I make sure there are peers in the room to help the student as necessary and I make it easy for that child to succeed and then I move on.

I walk away from this because a lot of times, the worthlessness and helplessness is that the child wants attention. I want you to sit down with him or her and go through it and I am not going to do that. Another thing I do that I found appropriate to make things go right, make sure your kids know how to do it and after some relevant and limited choices − you have three choices today - you can do this and this or this − it's not you can do this or do nothing. I have said this right at the start I don't like dealing with tantrums, I don't do those. So this is your choice, this, this or this − okay that's what I tend to do with that helplessness.

Rob Plevin: Very good, I am actually going to pick up on two points that you have already said if I can. You mentioned the choices, the choices are so powerful for these kids when they feel stuck. If you stand over them and give them instruction to get on with their work, "come on I'm waiting for you!", and you are tapping your foot and you are looking at them, there is no way they are going to move forward, it's too oppressive for them.

But the language of choice lets you get your objectives met whilst not taking the sting out of instruction for them so, "Johnnie, do you want to use a blue pen or a black pen to get on with your work?" "Do you want me to help you or do you want Simon to help you do your work?" So you are making it very clear that the only choice really is to 'do your work' but you are giving them a little bit of choice, and then by giving them a little bit of time to think about that rather than standing over them − "I'm going to give you two minutes to think about that and get down to your next bit of work and I'll come back and see you so we are giving them a little bit of think time."

And finally you were talking about making it easier to succeed for them − that to me is the key − they need to feel a sense of success. Helplessness has been built up by failure after failure and although pandering to them is possibly the worst thing to do – it just makes them even more reliant on others – it is also bad to just leave them without sufficient help. after-all, we wouldn't ignore a child who was drowning – we'd help them but also teach them how to swim so they don't get in the situation again.

So let's make it easy to succeed by chunking the work up and I use something called Targets – it's basically just putting a mark on their work where you are wanting them to get down to in a certain time so "in the next five minutes you need to get down to here." Telling them specifically what question they need to get down to or which task they have to finish in a given amount of time because when we present them with a mass of work, you know "here's your work it's two pages and you need to finish it by the end of the lesson in an hour's time" – woah, that's too much! They need a small, achievable task that they can achieve in a given time frame.

Students who won't complete work in class

Once a student has actually made a start on their work it's clear that at least two of the big de-motivators - fear (of failing or of appearing to be a 'goody two shoes' in front of under-achieving peers) and inadequacy (feeling they lack the necessary skills to bother attempting the task) – no longer have influence. If they've made a start but not finished the work then clearly something else has gone wrong along the way.

It's a bit like starting off on a journey and then deciding you don't want to continue. You've gone to the trouble of packing your bag, getting in the car and starting off but then decide to pull over half way down the motorway. Was there too much traffic? Did you forget something and decide to concentrate on that instead? Did something go wrong with the car? Did something at the side of the road distract you? Did you get too tired and need a snooze? Did you decide to pick up a hitch-hiker and go off somewhere else? Or did you simply decide the destination probably wasn't somewhere you want to visit after all?

When students' efforts tail off during a lesson after the work is started it's probably down to one or more of the following:

- Being distracted by other students or outside interruptions.

- Losing interest in work that becomes repetitive or too easy.

- Getting frustrated with work that becomes too difficult. (If they aren't gaining a sense of achievement they will soon switch off – remember how important 'empowerment' is?)

- Something going wrong with the equipment they're using which breaks their concentration and takes them out of 'work mode'.

- Discomfort – is the room too warm and stuffy? Is it too cold? Is there a bad smell floating around? (If you're teaching teenage boys it's highly likely).

- Waning energy, becoming lethargic.

- Finding that other students are getting all the attention. (They may feel the need to switch off/act up to get some negative teacher attention if they see other students taking up the teacher's time by doing so).

As you can see there are several possible reasons. This list is by no means exhaustive, but each of those possible reasons has one thing in common – they can all be alleviated or prevented with good planning.

This is one area of motivation in which the teacher has a considerable amount of control. Getting them to start work is the biggest problem and once they've actually made a start, keeping them working can be achieved simply by pre-empting the reasons above.

So how do you plan ahead for students who lose their motivation to work during lessons despite having made a reasonable start?

1. Take efforts to minimise and prepare for distractions.
Distractions can take many forms – some avoidable, some not – but there are ways we can reduce chances of occurrences and minimise their effects. Here are a few common distractions and ways to deal with them:

Distraction #1: Farting: Boys will be boys, and some of them (and rugby-playing girls) seem to take great delight in farting during lessons, usually when everyone in the room is silent - for extra comic effect. We can't control what he eats beforehand but we can reduce the chances of this happening by giving the boy sufficient attention so he doesn't feel as much need to cause a disruption. We should also have a good plan in place to deal with this particular distraction when it does occur. Iron-clad consequences are the best way.

Teacher: *Tommy we don't do that in lessons. Please pack up your things and move to the seat at the back. If it happens again you'll go to Time Out (or come back at break for five minutes – whatever sanction you have in place.)*

Tommy: *I couldn't help it.*

Teacher: *That may be true Tommy but it's something we have to learn to control. Move now please or, as I said, you'll be going to Time Out.*

The trick, as with any confrontation like this, is to show as little emotion as possible, not get drawn into a discussion or argument and to follow up EVERY time.

If you don't know who the culprit was you use a slightly different plan. Open a window, show as little concern as possible and tell students who are overreacting to be quiet and stop being silly. Have an activity on hand with which to re-focus them.

NB: No matter how earnest the protest that they 'couldn't help it' I would always assume it was deliberate and issue the consequence. Once you allow leeway for an 'accident' the rest have a perfect excuse for a repeat performance.

Distraction #2: Asking to go to the toilet: This is the favoured 'work-avoidance' strategy in many classrooms and you're going to have to have a plan for dealing with it. My personal view is that anyone can hold on for an hour (the duration of most lessons) and if they can't, they need to learn how to. I know there has to be provision made for some individuals on health grounds but unless they have a note from parents and/or the school has been made aware of this problem, all students should receive the same consideration. They are given opportunity to go to the toilet before the lesson starts and then nobody goes during the lesson. If that's too draconian for you, you can try being lenient on a student who claims they about to 'wet themselves' and then come up with another plan to deal with the five students who say they have the same problem ten minutes later. It is better to have one rule, and stick to it.

If you're worried about denying students their rights and receiving formal complaints from parents there are other alternatives such as issuing 'toilet passes' or setting a limit of one toilet visit per lesson per student, and recording visits in a file or the back of the student's book. In each case the student should be given a definite time by which they should be back in the room (written in their book/on the card) and they should take this with them. This will enable other staff such as tutors and other teachers to monitor trends – as well as preventing the student from being wrongly accused of wandering if caught in the corridor.

Distraction #3: Peers: This is easy to prevent and deal with. Separate students who are likely to distract each other. Move the liveliest students to the front of the room so you can keep a close eye on them. Have back-up/alternative lesson tasks on hand to re-focus students who lose concentration.

2. Plan for students getting bored or frustrated. Have frequent changes of task (every 15-20 minutes – less with low ability groups) and/or increasingly higher levels of challenge for able students, with simpler alternatives for less able. Prepare tasks which meet different learning styles and know your students so that you can offer them targeted work which is likely to introduce quick 'teach-back' and discussion activities to break monotony. Remember, once they switch off, it's going to be tough getting them switched on again – you must plan ahead and pre-empt boredom. As soon as you detect the warning signs act quickly to keep them on task. That's the time to change the activity, have a quick energiser or just offer them some quiet encouragement or support.

3. Make sure equipment is working properly and that you are able to quickly remedy it if something goes wrong. Have spare photocopies, pens, a back-up demonstration (or a technician on stand-by), calculators, batteries, discombobulators (applicable only in lessons on discombobulation) - in fact, spare versions of all the materials and equipment the students are going to be using. When something goes wrong you want to be able to hand them a solution without a pause.

4. Make sure the room is comfortable. Ensure that you are able to control things like temperature; ie that you know how to alter the lighting/use the air conditioning.

5. Have a resource bank of energisers and fill-in activities. You need a stock of these – good, fun fill-ins and active energisers which students enjoy – as a means to get them on their feet and quickly inject some oxygen into their lungs. You have no control over their sleeping habits or the fact that Jonny was up until 4am playing on his Xbox and can barely keep his eyes open... but you can inject some energy and liven him up a bit every fifteen or twenty minutes with a quick energiser. You can find plenty via Google or in some of our other titles - **'The Fun Teacher's Tool Kit' & 'The Active Teaching Tool Kit'** – both available on Amazon.

6. Keep them on task with encouragement and praise. I've mentioned this a lot elsewhere on the Behaviour Needs website so I'll not go into it too much here, other than to repeat that this is one of your most powerful tools – when it is used properly. Remember firstly that your words of encouragement must be sincere and that many of your students respond better to quiet, private encouragement. Enough said.

7. Give them a Target. Targets are so important for re-engaging a student who is just starting to waver. Let's say you have a student who's messing around, off task being mildly disruptive. It may well be that he's just not clear about what he's supposed to be doing, he may be confused, he may have misheard or he may just be a bit bored. An excellent tip for getting this student back on task is to define a very clear work target for him to achieve, and a set time in which to do so...

"Tony, this is your target – I want you to get to number 6 by half past ten."

(This is said very quietly so as not to disrupt the pace of the lesson or raise the attention of other students).

The target gives them something to work towards and reminds them you're supporting them – it shows them that you're interested in them and care about their progress. It gives them very clear instructions as to how to succeed in your lesson.

Boys in particular, work much better when they know exactly what is expected of them and some students can only cope with small chunks of work at a time. Target setting is perfect for achieving both these aims and can have a magical calming effect on most students who are starting to play up.

I use this method with all my classes. Once I've given them their tasks I go round and put a pencil mark where I expect them to get to in a set time.

"By ten past 11 Sarah you need to have completed the work to this mark – that's your target."

It's best to do this quietly because some students are self-conscious about having smaller targets than others and for others, the fact that I give them more work as their target can lead to quarrels.

Once you've done this a few times they get used to it and accept their individual targets quite happily. In fact, most lessons I have students actually asking me to give them a target!

In every class there are very badly behaved students who are, in fact very capable. With such children I explain, in private, that I'll be giving them a bigger target (more work) than anyone else. If I did this without explanation there would be an uproar, but by taking the student to one side before the lesson and quietly saying something along the lines of ...

"Shaun, I'm going to set you a high target today because I know you can excel at this. I wouldn't be doing my job right if I didn't give you the chance to show me what you can do. – OK?"

I normally get a very focused, hard-working student from then on. Try it for yourself.

Dealing with unmotivated students

[Questions from the Real World]

Andy Vass

Question: What are the best ways to motivate and inspire students?

Andy Vass: You can't motivate other people. What we do as teachers is we create the conditions where children can feel motivated and feel inspired. So we can't directly motivate others – it's about influence – so what is one of the best ways to inspire?

So if you want kids to feel inspired be inspirational, if you want kids to be motivated, be motivated about what you do. Generate a lot of positive relationships and remember the humanity of motivation and inspiration. Human beings by enlarge are always more significantly influenced by people that make them feel good so use a lot of modelling.

Relationships, I think Rob said this at some point, – relationships are based on 2 things essentially. One is to demonstrate that you really care and the other one is communicate effectively and frequently. I don't know if any of you have got a Visa card – probably lots of you – but the guy that started the Visa Corporation said that 90% of motivation and inspiration influence can be achieved by doing the following things – get two bits of paper – on the first write down everything that has been done to you that you hated, that made you small, that made you inhibited, that minimised your potential, that made you less of who you really are and make sure that you never do it to anybody else.

On the second piece of the paper write down everything that got you to close to your potential, or past your potential and make sure you give those things to other people.

Here are some keys to motivation...

1. Frequency of feedback. That's being really good giving lots of descriptive feedback, tell them what they are doing, tell them how to do it even better and scaffold between the two.

2. High challenge, low stress is a great motivator. When we present materials to them which are too challenging it de-motivates. When we present the materials that are too easy that de-motivates. High challenge, low stress and given choice and control that's a great motivational thing.

3. People strive for autonomy. It's a very powerful human need so allow them to make choice and control over how they present, how they find stuff out, and give them the responsibility. Have you come across something called WIIFM – What's in it for me? – so make sure the students have cleared their negotiated goals, make sure we use their imagination to how good they can be and make sure we are connecting them to hope because without hope there is nothing.

Students who won't complete homework

Getting students to complete homework is a typical problem for teachers – especially with students who lack motivation. If they're not working in class where we can stand over them, they certainly aren't going to work at home. Here are six ways to encourage students to complete and return their homework – and none of them involve you dishing out a never-ending stream of detentions or making promises of certificates and other treats (a.k.a. 'Bribes'!)

1. Make sure the work appeals to them – It sounds obvious but the more appealing you can make your homework in terms of having sufficient challenge, interest and practical value, the more chance your students will attempt it. With competitors like television, games, friends and the now-ubiquitous Facebook, if they see no point in it or if it's too boring/dull/easy it's obviously not going to appeal. As a long term strategy, if students gain a sense of pride and accomplishment when they finish work, they are more likely to attempt future tasks.

2. Make it achievable – Ideally it should be continuation of class work (rather than introducing something new) so they know how to do it. They need to know exactly what they're aiming for and what the finished product should look like. There's no point in giving them something they haven't a clue about, it just won't get done.

3. Include an element of choice – Choice is an incredibly powerful motivator so it should be included in homework tasks. Give them a choice of task ('any 3 tasks from the following 5') or a choice in the presentation method – 'produce a mind-map, report, illustration, magazine article or model' etc. (See 'Creative Homework Assignments' in resource area/cd).

4. Write it down – Always make sure students have the task (and any helpful instructions) written down clearly before they leave the room or post the task up on a blog/website so that they can access it any time. It cuts out the 'I didn't know what to do' excuses and provides them with a reminder should they get stuck

5. Include group interaction – We know that students like to work together so there is some merit in the idea of occasionally (or even regularly if it proves successful) setting a project which requires students to work in groups for completion. The individual accountability from peers involved in group work gives extra impetus to get the task completed

6. Get parents/carers involved – If you have children you're no doubt fully aware how much of a problem the whole issue of homework can cause at home. Parents do the cajoling, reminding, threatening, punishing and bribing while kids do the lying, avoiding, promising, making excuses and delaying. In many homes World War III breaks out over this single issue almost every night while in others it isn't even mentioned. With this in mind, many parents/carers (even those that appear totally unsupportive) will welcome help & direction from school on the subject of homework and this can be a very effective way of gaining their support in return.

If you have trouble getting support from some parents the key is to convince them that you are trying to help them and their child and make life easier for all. You don't want to come across as if this is for your benefit or to meet school targets.; rather, it's to help their child progress, succeed and do well. You need to show them how a little bit of support from them is going to have a dramatic effect on their child's progress in school and consequently on home life – happier child, easier life, fewer arguments, fewer detentions, fewer requests to visit school for a 'little chat' etc. (See 'Sample Homework Letter To Parents' & 'Ten Tips For Parents To Help With Homework' in Behaviour Tool Kit Appendix)

Begin by explaining to parents that homework involves the efforts of three separate parties – school, child, home – and that each party is dependent on support and input from the other two if the system is to work properly. Show them a record of any homework tasks that have been missed and explain the school policy and procedure for dealing with missed homework. Show them that it is neither pleasant nor beneficial for the student. If possible show them statistics for the effect of missed homework on overall grades.

Then show them the specific things they can do to help together with the days/times when this should happen. They'll need a copy of the homework schedule showing the days the work has to be handed in together with the suggested time to be spent on a task. Setting a regular, definite block of time – say 4:30-5:30pm – helps teach them time management.

Try to encourage them to set a time early on in the evening so that a) the child is still fairly alert and b) X Factor hasn't started. The idea is to create a habit, a routine which doesn't interfere with evening entertainment too much.

Another reason to set an early time is that it enables consequences to be brought into play . If homework is allowed to be last thing at night and the child is allowed to play on a computer or watch TV all night before that, how can consequences be applied?

They'll need a list of necessary materials and supplies to make available at home (in some cases the school could supply these) and you could even provide them with a set of 'parent notes' for a task the child is likely to find challenging so that they can take part and provide some assistance and instruction. I've dealt with many parents with severely academic limitations and they were delighted when I gave them these.

Finally, they may benefit from some behaviour management guidance in terms of suitable consequences such as withholding TV/computer game/mobile phone/pocket money until homework is completed. The easier you can make it for them to take part, the better the chances they will.

Whenever we've done this in schools the feedback from both the parent and the child has been very positive – parents enjoy spending some quality time with a child they have possibly had very little quiet contact with for a long time, while the students start to enjoy a sense of achievement as well as increased parental contact/attention.

[Questions from the Real World]

LouAnne Johnson & Rob Plevin

Question: Do you have any suggestions on motivating students with chaotic home lives and chaotic backgrounds to do homework?

LouAnne: There are two issues here. People have chaotic personal lives they come into the classroom and they are upset so I think it's important to have something in place so that when they come into the classroom, it's calming.

Whether you do a breathing exercise or some sort of physical activity or whether you do a journal write, so long as it is some type of stability. I like to do the journals because it gives them a chance to vent – they can write whatever they want in the journal, if they don't want me to read it they can throw it away or they can leave it for me to answer personally. And that was one way where I really got to help a lot of kids. Obviously I am not a therapist or a police officer - I cannot go and fix their lives but I can say, "I hear you, I understand you, let's focus on trying to help you make it through school so that you can then go create the kind of life you want and we'll try and find some resource to help you cope with what you are dealing with now."

Kids don't do homework for a lot of reasons but a lot of kids don't do it because they don't really know how to do it. They are used to copying off other people or it's just not a priority for them. I started having a 'homework lottery' because I look at the number of adults who will spend a dollar or more every day on a lottery ticket so I thought, "Ok well they like the idea of a chance."

So in my classroom when they bring their homework in and they have done it themselves and I know who has, then I will put that student's name in the 'homework lottery jar' and then randomly I pull out a name and that person wins something.

They don't know whether they are going to win a pencil or if they are going to win a Walkman. I am not saying I buy them but I go round to businesses and I ask for donations, people giving me CD'S, DVD'S, Backpacks, Books whatever I have – a lot of fast-food places will give you coupons I don't like to give those away but it's still food, if somebody is starving I'd rather them eat junk than nothing so then I will give them a reward so they never know.

All you have to do is give away a couple of really good prizes a couple of times and people will start bringing in their homework. Now does that actually motivate them? I really don't know. Is it motivating them to learn or is it just motivating them to try and win the prize?

If you are a math's teacher and you say, "Ok do the odd question at the end of the chapter" then a lot of students aren't going to be motivated to do that. If you say, "I want you to look at the questions at the end of the chapter and I want you to make up two of your own problems, bring them in tomorrow and we'll share them," that's a whole different thing.

Rob: Can we take that a little further? I was working in the Arab Emirates last year and there's a big problem over there with kids who have everything; some are very spoilt over there see no point in doing work. In fact, the message from their parents is that they don't need to work. Solomon has asked a question in the question box in relation to these students. 'How can we motivate them to do their homework?'

LouAnne: I think we have to question is this homework really going to be helpful or is it just something that I need for a grade? My question is, Is it really important for them that they show their work? Maybe so then give them 50% if they can't show it but sometimes I don't think the homework is actually challenging or worthwhile.

Rob: With a couple of my students who were reluctant to complete homework I realised it was largely because they lacked the organisational & time management skills (as well as the resources and materials) to actually do the work at home. Their lives are chaotic – they get home, watch TV or whatever and don't make time for the work because it's not made a priority in the home.

So I sat down with them & we started looking at managing their evening - where they could slot in 15 – 30 minutes – timetabling their other activities so that they weren't missing out on anything. Then we talked about all the benefits to them of getting the homework out of the way and then and making sure they had the resources – pens etc. that they needed. They really appreciated that extra bit of time that I was taking and once they had those skills with which to do their homework then their chances of doing it were greatly increased and in fact that did solve the problem, they started bringing their homework in. How many times do we get at these kids and say, "You haven't bought your homework in – you've got yourself a detention"? And we're all about punishing them without taking into account the fact that they haven't got the skills that they need.

LouAnne: That is a really great point. We could put students in small groups and say, "I have a problem people – homework isn't being completed. I need your advice on how we can change this." and let them tell you.

Enjoying this book so far? I'd love it for you to share your thoughts and post a quick review on Amazon!

Just head over to Amazon, search for the book title and click on the 'Write a customer review' button!

Behaviour-related problems

Managing girls' behaviour

[Questions from the Real World]

Julia Thompson & Rob Plevin

Question: Recently two girls have been transferred to my year 10 class and they have created havoc. About ten people in this class have developed a mentality and they are making hell for the rest of us. Literally I am sure they are ten of them who not only refuse to be removed from the room but refuse to be stood down from the school from their principles – these girls are horrible.

Julia Thompson: OK you know what I am going to tell you works for me and honestly this is so weird because I would do this again. Here's what worked...

I always try and look at the cause of the problem and what this is it is a power struggle, it is a two against one power struggle in that two girls are opposing the teacher so what happened in my classroom was I actually had a mother come to school and smack a student out in the hallway. The whole time shouting at her – it was awful. So what happened was I divided my class into two groups to work on a big project where they wrote things to help the community, so they were doing good in the world, like the freerice.com – so I divided them and each one headed up part of the class so it was a competition so instead of opposing me they were opposing each other.

In a friendly positive manner they got to be leaders, they focused on opposing each other trying to beat each other, competing with each other in each other's group, they did it in a positive way because it was something good to do and so because they were focused on each other – it is basically a divide and conquer sort of thing, instead of struggling against me they got me to be their ally when they were working on this competition. I can't remember what the competition was, but they worked to do something good, they got other people to join in. These girls are good at getting people to join them, so use that to your advantage. Whenever they have that kind of power make them use it for good and turn it away from you by being a co-operative kind teacher. Then focus on good things that they do and re-direct that energy.

Rob Plevin: In the UK we have a TV programme called 'The World's Strictest Parents' and the way it works is that they pick two really tough teenage kids who are really struggling at home and it shows them in their own homes where they are abusing the parents - you know beating them up and spitting at them and all kinds of really horrible things. They show these kids meeting their new 'parents' – a couple they'll be staying with for a week or two - and you see the kids behaving terribly from the outset and the producers make you think 'there's no way these people can possibly change this kid in such a short time them'. But they do - they turn them round and get a transformation every time.

What they do is about halfway through the week they take them to some kind of setting, be it a hospital, an old people's home or a centre for kids who are disabled and they introduce the kids as helpers. They get them to help out for these people and every single time those kids end up in tears saying, "I never realised people were so badly off compared to me." And they change virtually in an instant. There is this human need to contribute, to help other people and to feel that connection to be wanted and useful and if you can harness that as you have explained there Julia I think we are on a winner.

Classroom management for supply/substitute teachers

[Questions from the Real World]

Julia Thompson & Rob Plevin

Question: How can we get the substitute/supply teacher to gain respect in the classroom?

Julia Thompson: I love this question, I was a substitute teacher for two very long years at fifteen dollars per day and I know the answer to this. First of all you are not going to get respect right away, it comes with exposure.

So that's one thing and another thing is make sure when you go to school you definitely need to have a bagful of extra stuff for students to do. So you can pull down some puzzles go to puzzlemaker.com and make a bunch of classroom puzzles. Have plenty for them to do because honestly there is nothing more annoying than a teacher who said....oh show them a video and the video doesn't show. Then you are stuck with a classroom full of people who are ready to drive you mad.

The next thing I would suggest for every substitute/supply teacher is to get to school early and make sure you ask questions – go bug everybody, I mean what have you got to lose? You know these are not people who you know, who you work with every day, ask them to make sure you have got everything what to do and if a person doesn't like your plans make sure the office knows about that – so that you can get those plans.

And then the most important thing you have to actually remember to get respect is no matter what, do not lose your cool. Because that is the one thing that students are hoping and praying for all day long, that you are going to make some enormous scene. Whatever you do don't do that. Act like you are confident, act like you know what you are doing and it's going to work out – I believe that.

Rob Plevin: Just to pick up on that, one thing to turn them off you straightaway is to go in with guns blazing isn't it? They don't know you and they are tuned in to try and wind you up as a sub. If you go in screaming and shouting and trying to lay the law down straightaway you have put that barrier up between you and them and it can be really difficult from then on.

The one thing I would say that helped me most when I was working as a substitute was to get to know them as quickly as possible. It all starts with relationships – so rather than going straight into curriculum, start with some 'getting to know you' activities, start with some games, it gets you off on the right foot and it gets it off to a positive start. You never see any kind of therapist who is working with a new client working their magic on them until they have got to know something about them first.

You need to have that relationship in place and if you can, learn their names. In fifteen minutes it can be done , you can have a class set of names in fifteen minutes if you concentrate on it and boy that works just like magic. When you start calling them all by their first names ten or fifteen minutes after first meeting them they are AMAZED. It is an instant bridge-builder and it shows them you are interested in them.

Here's a quick tip for doing that... First draw up a seating plan. You need one student you can trust to back up the seating plan too so that you know it matches up with the register – you know, so you know that you are not getting false names. You draw up a plan of the classroom with all the students' first names in place at each desk/table.

Then you get them engrossed in a simple activity that isn't going to take any input from you just for five or ten minutes and while their heads are down that's when you go around the seating plan matching their names to their faces. And really it's easy enough to do this but when you focus on a small task like that it's surprising how quick those names go in and if you then spend another ten minutes on the lesson here and there by the end of the lesson you can just ream off all their names – it may not work the first time, but very rarely has it gone beyond the whole lesson for me. I can usually learn a class of names in ten minutes – anyone can, if they focus on it.

The trick lies in the matching of their names to their faces. I have an info sheet on this in our Behaviour-ology.com resource area but it basically boils down to fixing an image in your mind that links to their name. So, for instance, if I was trying to remember a student called 'Rob' I would look at his face and imagine him either dressed as a 'Robber' – you know in a stripy jumper, carrying a 'swag bag' – or perhaps dressed in a kilt with a big sword – like 'Robert the Bruce'. Whatever, you just try to make the image as crazy as possible – it's much easier to remember funny images. Try it, it works.

Julia Thompson: Oh you are absolutely right Rob. Let me tell you what I do as a teacher to make life easier for my substitutes. First of all I photograph all my students in their correct configuration and so I tend to change their desks periodically so I get outside my camera and photograph my students and I print it out and so I write their names underneath their photograph like a photograph of everybody in the room where they are supposed to be and I write their names on it. So I then put it in a folder for my substitute so that the substitute will know what's going on and who is supposed to be sitting where. So that helps too. I try to make it easy for my substitutes but all my students seem to lose their instruction time.

[Questions from the Real World]

LouAnne Johnson

Question: As a supply (substitute) teacher do you have any suggestions for building rapport with students?

LouAnne: Yes I think this is important as you have the plan of what you are going to do when you go into the room so it's your agenda, not theirs. You want to take something like an icebreaker – a 5 or 10 minute activity - you will get the chance to get to know the kids a little bit and you can go right into the lesson that the teacher has planned. But I would have some other lesson planned just in case that one is too easy or too hard or you are missing paperwork or whatever – it's going to happen.

Another thing that I do before I go in I go to an attendance of one of the counsellors and I look at the role sheet for the class and I say, "Who here might be somebody trustworthy so they could help me?" You don't want to ask for a volunteer to take the role because some kids will do that but some will pretend to be someone else, so I ask some of the adults who I can ask, and of course I am not going to recall that name out and say that the adults recommended them because that makes them the Brownie but I would not go in and start taking role because number one, you don't know who they are so you don't know if they are telling the truth, and also when you are taking role they look like they're busy and you're occupied so that's not real class – that's when they can have their personal conversations.

You could have a copy of different optical illusions and you have four different optical illusions and you've made multiple copies so you just randomly pass them out and say, "Okay I would like you to find the person that has the same optical illusion that you have, that's your group and I want you guys to see if you can figure out why it works then I'll come around and ask your group." So they are immediately engaged in the optical illusion because even if they think they don't want to, as soon as they look at it their brain is going to be engaged.

Then you talk over why they are doing that and then you say, "Okay, let's see what your optical illusion is?" So you've taken the focus from you, and put it on to them, got their brains engaged, you've got your role taken and your ready to go – they gave you the chance to get the lesson started. So I learned the hard way – it's not to go in and start taking the role and start to shuffle papers around.

[Questions from the Real World]

Angela Watson & Rob Plevin

Question: How do you motivate a class with extreme behaviours when they are not your class? How do you get over the "Let's see how far we can push the supply teacher stage?"

Angela: This is a very special scenario and I think one of the most important things you can do is stay calm no matter what. The energy and attitude that you project really makes a big difference as to how students perceive and respond to you. Pick your battles very carefully and remember it's only for one day, the same way that you as a parent don't treat other peoples' children up to the same high standard as you do for your own children.

It's the same way when you are a substitute or a supply teacher. You don't have that kind of influence over their life, you don't have that sort of control as well, so just project an image to the students of being unflappable so that they know they are not going to be able to get you and after as well. Your job is to play the role of a well-balanced, calm, perfectly sane teacher even when you feel like you just want to scream and pull out your hair and run out of the classroom. Behave the way that you want to feel and your feelings will follow that. Pick your battles very carefully with them.

The exception is if you are in a long term assignment with the class, then I would advise you to establish your own reward system with the class set up your own procedures and routines, tell the kids that when the teacher comes back you'll do things her way; while I am here this is the way we are going to do it and then let's talk about why we are going to do it this way. So you are in charge, run the classroom as if it's your own if you are in a long term assignment.

Dealing with unsupportive parents

[Questions from the Real World]

Julia Thompson & Rob Plevin

Question: How do you deal with unsupportive parents?

Julia Thompson: I have said this before – make sure that everything you do is professional and above board and in line with your school's policies. So they can't help but support the school when they support you. Make sure that you don't deviate from what you are supposed to do. Make sure that everything you send home in writing is perfectly proof read. You are absolutely above board and you have that transparent professional demeanour with them. Everything you need to do is "let's work together" and to show them that you value their child.

But sometimes parents are just not able to or not willing to respond. Their economics are messed up because they haven't a job or they may have a negative view of education based on past experience. I would suggest that in every school you can never have strong enough parent support groups so might I suggest that you work with your individual student, see what you can do when you take on another task, this will strengthen things in your school to show that your school can draw parents in because you know really it is a school wide issue.

Rob Plevin: You picked up on a point there that for so many of them it is hard for them to make contact due to their background etc., and I think that is really the key point here.

When you are looking at unsupportive parents in many cases it could be that you have 3 or 4 generations who've had a really bad experience and when you are dealing with really challenging kids a lot of the contact that those parents have had with school has been very negative. So half the time they don't even want to pick the phone up because they are expecting more of the same.

Also in some cases you mentioned their economic issues. Maybe their educational issues too – lack of schooling etc. also impact and make them feel embarrassed about coming forward and making contact with school. I think the issue is to make it easy for them, give them as many ways as possible to get in touch with you rather than the usual – 'come into school for a meeting'. That may be too daunting at first.

People are using blogs, they are using text messaging – with the modern age of technology there are many ways they can get in touch with you in the first instance. So make yourself very, very welcoming and supportive first and foremost. If every contact you have with them is starting off about something negative about their kids, then the relationship with them is going to be very difficult to build up and it is the relationship again that is the key here.

Building up relationships with parents is much the same as building it up with the students. I will give you an example – I used to call my students' parents regularly, I would call each of them at least once a week and I would just have a two minute call just to let them know that their student had done something positive. I tried very hard to find something positive to say, I would call up and say, "Hi is that Mrs. Smith? I just want to let you know that Johnnie has been really good today in maths (or whatever it was) that's all I just wanted to let you know."

All those little two minute calls build up, gradually you begin to break down that cycle of them not wanting to hear from school and gradually they see that we are on their side. And you know what? A lot of them do seem very unsupportive at first but once we start to break that barrier down – they want the same things as all of us do for our kids, they want them to succeed, they want them to do well. It saddens me to think that so many relationships between school and home could so easily be formed (together with all the positive benefits that brings) just by making a few phone calls.

I once remember on a presentation at one of the schools I was working in, for students who had been excluded from mainstream school. And these kids had achieved pretty much nothing throughout their lives and we made sure that at this presentation every single one of them would receive a certificate and an award for something – even if it was something that most ceremonies like this would overlook. Do you know what? We got about 60% of the parents at that award ceremony and we had big burly guys turning up with tattoos and piercings all over and seven of them were in tears when they saw their kids get an award. I was talking to some of them afterwards and they were saying, "this is the first time he has been recognised for anything. I love my son and I'm so proud. Thank you!" It was incredibly moving to see that happening – these were parents who had been labelled as 'completely unsupportive'. I think the reality was that they were just beaten by the system, they had given up and just needed some hope, a little light in the tunnel, you know?

Now those two minute conversations, we can really turn them into a very powerful strategy by just finding out a little bit more about the parents when we are talking with them. Every now and again a little tip of information will come out like Mrs Smith will say, "We've got Grandma staying this week" or "Johnnie's sister has just had a baby." Those pieces of information are GOLD!

You need to write down and take a note of them because next time you call Mrs Smith (and by now you should be on first name terms), next time you call Pauline you can say, "by the way how is grandma?", or, "how is the baby doing? What has she called him? You'll have to bring him in to school to show us!" And every time you have a communication with them from then on they see that you are interested in them, and that is when your relationship starts to grow. Before long you have got somebody who is hyper-supportive because they see that you share that common goal with them of helping them and helping their child. It's not exactly rocket science but it works like magic.

Julia Thompson: You know Rob you use the word relationships several times and you can't be more on target. It is worth it to keep pushing, to keep trying and to build a better relationship.

Dealing with students who answer back

[Questions from the Real World]

Julia Thompson & Rob Plevin

Question: How can I get my disrespectful students not to answer back?

Julia Thompson: If you teach students as old as I do, they don't tend to answer back so much so they roll their eyes – and they give that horrible rolling look across the room – oh I just can't stand that. So this is what I suggest I have a bunch of suggestions here.

First of all when a student is rude to me I do something they don't expect and it throws them off. I tend to smile at them. I just have this huge smile on my face and at the time they are a little shocked, I never say "what did you just say?" because they will say the insult/comment again, so just smile at them.

I am never rude to them - I feel that if I am going to be rude to a student they are going to be rude back.

Sometimes I think they just don't know any better and so I try to ignore it at first so that maybe they said something odd or off-putting but if it continues then I take that student aside and very quietly I say "Hey, how could you have said that differently because to tell you the truth I think you don't know how much it means to me. But you hurt my feelings or that wasn't as nice as you could have put it, I don't think of you that way." I always say "you know, you're better than that."

I try to reduce guilt when I can to do that too. Sometimes a child just doesn't mean to be disrespectful, they get all caught up in the moment and then they just blurt something horrible out. That is a little bit different than when they are deliberately trying to provoke me so I might say "now if you really wanted to or intended to say something crude or rude or hateful to me I do treat that as a very serious problem." and then issue consequences as a response.

Rob Plevin: OK I will start off where you left there with the consequences. We have to have that final boundary but I am also going to say that there are so many things we can do before that.

First of all, asking 'why is it that they are being disrespectful to us?' 'Why is it that they are answering back?' can be a good place to start. A lot of the times, I am not saying every time, this could be down to the fact that the types of students that do this are motivated by a need for attention or a subconscious need for power. And we want to try and meet that need, or satisfy it, in an appropriate way, i.e. by giving them some sense of responsibility. By having a quiet chat with them and just explaining how you really could do with them on side, you can often achieve a lot more so with a quiet supportive chat rather than jumping in straight away with punishment.

Consequences have got to be there, no doubt, but there's a difference between having stepped, fair consequences in place and what some people do, which is to jump straight in with a punishment. And when kids hurt our feelings, when we have broken our backs to try and support them and trying to give them these great lessons we are trying to teach them, it does hurt when they answer back - and the immediate reaction can be to jump back in with something that is going to 'get them back'.

Sometimes the best reaction is not to have any reaction at all and just to step back and meet them with silence - that can be quiet unnerving for them and can really make them reflect on what they are doing. You picked up on some great points there about telling them "you know, I don't speak to you like this and I don't expect to hear you speaking to me like this."

Finally we can try and build up an atmosphere where we focus on the positive so rather than waiting for kids to do something wrong such as answer back, we are constantly reinforcing when students do it right. So thanking students when they are speaking politely - all those moments and there are so many of them - when kids do something right, when they put their hand up or when they just mention your name, or when they hold a door open - they are the sort of things we have got to reinforce and keep on mentioning to show students that that's what we are looking for, that's what we are focusing on.

Dealing with low-level disruption

This sort of disruption can be like water torture to the teacher, that incessant symphony of pencil tapping, silly noises, poking, bogey-flicking, giggling, inappropriate flatulence, paper-passing, ruler-slapping, desk shoving, hair-pulling, and general fidgeting.

Kids will be kids, and in themselves many of the above are all fairly harmless activities (though those involving bodily functions can be hard to stomach, and hair-pulling can really hurt). Taken collectively they are incredibly wearing and can make a teacher's life hell.

There are as many ways of dealing with low level disruption as there are types of disruption – from use of humour to thumb screws – but I'm going to give you a stepped script here which you may find handy because it can be used to address virtually any type of low-level interruption...

1. State what they are doing, and what you want them to do instead. The first thing to do is point out very clearly what they are doing wrong. It's surprising the effect this can have on them – sometimes they might not be aware how annoying their behaviour is for other people in the room until it is spelled out to them. In terms of what you want them to do you need to make their choices as simple as possible and leave no room for misunderstanding. You also need to explain why they should do what you're asking – ie, tell them what will happen if they don't follow your instructions. By doing this you show that you're not just getting on their backs just for the sake of it – there are reasons for your actions. This of course, gives them fewer excuses to complain or argue.

"John you're not doing your work and you're putting everyone off with that tapping. You need to pick your pen up and finish your target so that you don't have to get it finished in your own time."

If they don't immediately start doing as you've asked or if they answer you with a promise to do it soon, you should move on to stage 2. A promise that they will do as you ask 'in a minute' or 'later' is their way of trying to control the situation – so treat it as if they have ignored you and move to stage 2.

2. Explain exactly what will happen to them if they continue disrupting the lesson or ignoring you. Tell them very clearly what the sanction will be if they continue - clearly and without fuss or emotion. Avoid humour too, because by now they have crossed the line.

"If you don't stop throwing the bits of eraser you'll have to spend your break clearing the floor."

"If you don't manage to get the work finished, I'll get the boss of the internet to close Facebook down forever."

3. Give them time to think about your instruction. Immediately follow on by giving them a time limit and then back off, walk away and give them some space. Allow them to save face. It's hard for them to jump to attention and do what you want when you're standing over them, particularly if their friends are watching (and of course you know they are).

"I'm going to give you thirty seconds to do as I've asked."

"I'll be back in less than a minute and I expect to see it done."

It's all about telling them exactly where the boundary is and exactly what they have to do to get back on the right path. By backing off – walking to another part of the room or going to help another student - you're giving them a chance to back down without losing face; you're giving them an escape route. A child backed into a corner finds it difficult to back down in front of their classmates if you're standing over them and will react accordingly – usually with more defiance. By walking away you take the pressure off.

4. If they do as you've asked, acknowledge it. A few words is all that's needed to let them know they did the right thing and to encourage them to do it in future. It's a big step they've just taken. Don't lecture them about how they should follow instructions faster next time; just give them a sincere smile and some quiet private praise.

Younger students can be rewarded more formally – perhaps by giving them a sticker or a certificate for meeting the behaviour target 'Follow teacher's instructions'.

5. If they choose not to follow your instructions then you simply give them their consequence.

"Ok you've chosen to carry on doing...... That's fine. You'll be staying in at break for 5 minutes. Now get on with your work so that you don't lose any more of your time."

6. If the consequence has little or no effect. If the behaviour resumes after a few minutes respite, repeat the procedure with a tougher consequence this time: the next in your hierarchy. This is why you should always start off with a small consequence. If you wheel out your big guns straight away – threatening to switch on the portable mobile phone jammer instead of reducing break time by five minutes - you have no reserves if they continue to misbehave.

"John, if you don't stop talking I'm going to keep you behind for five minutes at break."

"You've already lost five minutes of your break, if you don't want to lose another five minutes you need to pick up the rubber you just threw."

"John, you're a rubbish shot, and that's your whole break gone, I warned you. Unless you want me to keep you behind after school I suggest you settle down and get the work finished."

Dealing with interruptions and constant chatter

A lesson doesn't necessarily have to be totally silent in order to be a success – unless you're Marcel Marceau - but if noise levels rise to the point where they are affecting others, it's time to take action. Here are some things to consider...

1. Assess your delivery. Have you been talking too long? Almost all my early lessons consisted of a relatively long, didactic introduction; I meant well and wanted to ensure everyone knew what they were doing but student attention spans are not known for their longevity and it is unrealistic to expect them to sit in silence listening for any more than a couple of minutes at a time.

Have you used intrigue to get their attention? Have you chopped the work up into focused, bite-sized sections? Have you included breaks and humorous energisers? Is the work achievable? Have you made it relevant to them? Have you tried to include topics they find interesting? Are you playing background music and changing the tune during transitions? Are you using active learning strategies to keep them engaged and on-task?

If they are chatting excessively it may be because the work and/or your delivery hasn't captured them.

2. Stop giving attention to those who are talking Instead, make positive statements about the behaviour you want to see:

"Thank you for your responses – I'll answer anyone who puts their hand up without calling out."

"Thanks to people on this table for raising your hands."

3. Try to deal with the problem positively

"You have a right to be heard - but you need to talk at the right time."

"You're a good talker, let's hear what you have to say about the work."

"You have a great speaking voice – we should use that – you can read the next chapter."

4. Alter seating plans Split the group into mixed ability groups to encourage peer support or partner the offending student with someone who can help keep them on task. Use choices to introduce the idea that a seating change is likely to happen if they continue talking.

"Paul, you can either carry on sitting where you are and work without talking - or you'll have to move to this chair at the front and work there without talking. The choice is yours."

5. Praise small steps and encourage more progress Either verbally or with a written note placed on their work:

"Thank you, you've been quiet for the last ten minutes – keep it up. Let's set a timer and see if you can get to the next ten minutes."

6. Adopt a no-nonsense approach Start with non-verbal gestures; hold your arm out, palm facing them as a 'stop' signal. If they continue, walk into their territory and put your hand on their desk or on their book to let them know you don't approve of them interrupting. If they persist, don't get wound up, just tell them you're bored and that their talking is preventing other people from learning. Then move on through your hierarchy of stepped consequences.

[Questions from the Real World]

Fintan O'Regan

Question: How can I help the children to listen to an explanation which they need to have understood before attempting the task?

Fintan: Again a lot of this is going to depend on the age and stage of the child we are talking about but if you are trying to get a child with ADHD to try and listen while you are explaining something to them, the obvious thing that many of you do is that you break it down into chunks. "If you do that this will happen", you always structure it in a sentence, you certainly wouldn't do it like I am talking in this lecture, you break it down into chunks, bullet points.

You may well have them writing it down as you are doing it, so that they can refer to their list of instructions (or you could give them a copy of the instructions, of course). I think the key thing is if you are doing it you also use your voice - lower your voice at different points, use your tone that you can emphasise certain things in that way.

You could also make sure that you had the child sat beside another student who acts as a re-enforcer. You have got other students in your class that can help you do the job by explaining the instructions to the student in question or can even ensure that they remain quiet while you are talking. Ring-leaders are excellent to use in this role because they also benefit from, and appreciate, the responsibility you're giving them.

When you do that you will actually increase your time to teach those other students; it makes sense.

Dealing with a chatty, noisy group

[Questions from the Real World]

Angela Watson

Question: How do you set and maintain appropriate noise levels in a year 5 classroom? I basically have a great class with no behaviour issues, what tricks can I use to get them to use a quiet indoor voice? It isn't even that they are off task they are just loud.

Angela: Great question. When kids get really involved in their activity they forget to monitor their volume and that actually is quite a good thing because they are focussed. First of all adjust your expectations on what your classroom is supposed to sound like and if it really is just too loud for you or maybe some of the kids, have a class discussion about it, talk about the problem, ask the kids what their solutions would be. Say, "You kids are doing this activity and I see how focussed you are, but it really hurts my ears because there are so many people talking at once so what can you do about it?" You are just sharing with the kids how you feel and this makes it a more sensitive to the issue.

You could also use concrete reminders or clues to help kids monitor their volume. One thing I found is turn the music on softly whilst the kids are working and if the kids can't hear it that's how they know they are too loud. If they can hear the music then the volume is okay.

Another option which you could use in the situation where the volume just feels out of control - have some sort of noise meter on the board. You can draw something or make a little poster that has a couple of different levels maybe green means appropriate levels, yellow means getting a little bit too loud, orange is louder and then red is way too loud.

Each time you ordinarily nag kids to be quiet, walk over to the poster, move the clip up one level to indicate that you have given them a noise level reminder and then go back to your task, go back to whatever you were doing, helping kids that are working with the small group creating papers, whatever you were doing. Don't say a word just move it and the kids will know this and they will prompt each other, they will say, "Sssh you're making a noise, she's moving the noise meter."

You know how kids get they will pay attention and they'll remind each other. So you don't have to say a word. If it gets loud again move it up to the next level and then the third or fourth time or how many warnings you decide to give them – just say very calmly, "The activity has to end now you are going to have to work independently without talking to each other and go ahead and clean up." The kids will realise it's not a punishment it's just a natural consequence for the choices they made. So making a visual reminder like that puts the ball back in their court to monitor their own behaviour and lets them know that if they can't then the consequence will be they won't be able to continue the activity in the same way.

How to get any class quiet in 15 seconds or less

This is a very simple classroom management strategy taken from my main classroom management title, 'Take Control of the Noisy Class.' I often used this in class when I was a teacher, and now use at seminars and workshops to demonstrate the power of giving students responsibility for their own behaviour. Not only can this technique get a rowdy group of students quiet in as little as 15 seconds, it also strengthens staff/student relationships, injects a little humour into the session and gives challenging students the attention they crave. It also works equally well with 8 year olds, 18 year olds, and even 63 year olds (I haven't gone higher than that!).

Indeed, it is so effective that at a recent teacher training seminar in Dubai I overheard some of the participants talking during the break and one of them remarked...

"He just got a room of 150 rowdy students quiet in 5 seconds!"

This is how I did it... it relies on two key principles:

1. Responsibilities

2. Routines

Some of your students will respond very well to being given a responsibility. In fact, it's probably your most challenging students, the ring leaders, who will respond best to responsibility because they crave attention so much. A great way to give them this attention (in a very positive way) is to give them a job, and for this classroom strategy we are going to award three or four students with the job of getting the rest of the class quiet.

These students are going to be our **'Shushers'** and it is their responsibility to 'shush' the rest of the class members (in a special way) when asked to do so.

To give them every chance of success we are going to train them. Each nominated 'Shusher' is asked to give their best and loudest 'Shush' – complete with an angry scowl and finger on lip gesture. After a few practices the 'Shushers' are then told that whenever the teacher shouts out "Shushers!" they are to give their best and loudest 'Shush' in unison. The rest of the class are told that when they hear the Shushers shush, they must stop talking and sit in silence. After two or three practices, they all get the idea and we now have the makings of a very effective routine in place.

To give the shushing routine the best chance of success there are three additions which I have found to be useful. Firstly, your Shushers need regular feedback. They need to be told when they are doing a good job and given hints and pointers when they are slacking or messing around. Both positive and constructive feedback should be given in private, out of earshot of other students. Remember that the students you use as Shushers are likely to be natural livewires so they will need careful management to make sure they continue to do a good job.

Secondly, I like to give each of my Shushers a uniform to wear so that they can be easily identified. The 'uniform' is actually just a silly hat or joke school cap but they love wearing them, even though I'm not entirely sure why. Maybe it makes them feel special, maybe it just makes the whole affair less serious but whatever the reason, it works.

Finally, I have found that Shushers sometimes need a little extra help to get a particularly rowdy class to settle. I give them this by using another routine prior to calling on them – the Countdown:

"10... You should all be sat on your own seats now with your bags away and your hands on the table... excellent Carly and Sophie, you got it straight away.

9... Brilliant over here on this table let's have the rest of you doing the same.

8... You need to finish chatting, get that mess away and be sat facing me.

7... All done over there at the back, well done, just waiting for a few others.

6... Come on, still some bags out at the back and people talking.

5... Good

4...

3... We're just waiting for one group now. Ah, you've got it now and you're sitting perfectly, thank you.

2... Well done everyone, nearly there...

1... Brilliant"

Pause

"Shushers!"

The countdown is a proven classroom management strategy for getting students quiet at the end of an activity or session and it creates a settled environment so that the 'Shushers' only then need to deal with the minority who are still talking.

So there you have it. A great way to get rowdy groups of students settled in record time. Enjoy.

Dealing with latecomers and poor punctuality

Here is a selection of strategies and creative ideas for preventing the problem of punctuality - plus a complete, step-by-step plan for dealing with students arriving late.

1. Have clear rules and consequences in place. Having students wander into class late is a common problem, particularly as they get older, but you can do much to prevent it by having clear, consistent rules on punctuality backed up by cast-iron consequences. Students need to know exactly what will happen if they are late and that consequences will be applied every time, regardless of the excuse the student uses.

Consequences can form part of a hierarchical plan - from the two minute follow-up (explained below) to time made up after school and contact with parents for more serious cases - or they can be more humorous such as inviting students who are not in their seats when the bell rings to go to the front of the room and sing a song. As a colleague who favoured the humorous approach once told me:

"Sometimes there are two students wandering in late so we have a duet and occasionally even a choir. It puts a smile on everyone's face and starts the class in an upbeat way. And surprisingly, punctuality is not the issue it used to be since I started using this strategy!"

2. Reward those who are on time. Students like to do well and good attendance is something that all students can achieve, regardless of ability; it should be acknowledged like any other social skill.

Recognition can take the form of verbal or written praise, a special award or more formal rewards such as free time. Explain to students that you will allocate them 3 minutes of 'wasted time' each day. They can use up that time each day or save it up and use it for something special.

Agree on something students could do with the 'wasted' time such as watching a video, playing a game or having a popcorn party and decide how much time they will need to save for that special event. Tell students that as soon as they've saved the required amount of time, they will be able to hold their special event.

When they waste time during the day, start a stopwatch, time the amount of time wasted, and subtract it from the three minutes. Inter-class competition between groups on this issue is also a good motivator.

3. Surprise, surprise! Punctuality and attendance can be encouraged in a fun way by randomly choosing one student's desk or chair each day and placing a sticker or note beneath it. The student who arrives (on time) to find the sticker under his or her seat gets to choose a small prize. If the student is absent or late, the prize is forfeited or cancelled (or perhaps it's "clean the toilets – with a toothbrush!").

A step-by-step classroom management plan for dealing with latecomers...

i). Give latecomers as little attention as possible. Calmly, and without fuss, take their name (assuming you don't already know it) and confirm that they are late:

"John, you're ten minutes late...."

ii). Direct them to their seat. Quickly direct them to a seat and give them something to occupy them – they could watch the remainder of an explanation/demonstration or get on with a worksheet or written task while you concentrate on the other learners. Don't ask them why they're late at this stage because this will cause disruption to the lesson flow and shift focus where you don't want it. They will be given opportunity to explain their reason for being late in the 'two-minute follow-up' after the lesson, explained below.

"...Sit there please and get on with (insert task), you can explain why you're late after the lesson."

iii). Praise those who are working. Take the focus off the latecomer by giving positive attention to those who are working.

"Excellent work you two, nice to see you getting on with that."

iv). Address latecomers separately once other students are settled. Once the majority of the students are working the next step is to get the latecomer/s engaged properly in the lesson task. This can be done by either gathering them as one group and giving them the full demonstration/lesson introduction again or (better) pair them up with other students who can teach them or explain the task to them.

v). Follow up with latecomers at the end of the lesson. Students who were on time can, if feasible and appropriate, be given a slightly early finish to enable you to follow up for no more than two minutes with those who were late (see the 'two-minute follow-up' below).

vi). Keep thorough records. Get latecomers to fill in a form giving reason for late arrival and the time they arrived. Send copies home with notification of consequences if it continues.

vii). If students are absent... when work sheets are distributed, place copies in folders for absentees. At the end of the day, simply label each folder with the absent students' names so that missed work is ready for their return.

Dealing with abusive language/swearing

Children need to be very clear about the consequences of their use of bad language. If there is no school policy in place then use your own - and stick to it. That way they will eventually learn that they cannot get away with it.

The oft-quoted strategy of staying calm applies equally well here. No matter how profane the offence (and you don't need me to tell you how creative they can be), try not to lose your temper. Let your chosen consequence do the job for you. Calmly state 'that's a minute you owe me' (or whatever your sanction is for this scenario), mark it down, and carry on with the lesson. Don't raise your voice while doing this as that can be read as the emotional response they are probably trying to trigger.

If swearing is a regular occurrence the consequence needs to begin quite small. That may sound like double-dutch but if the air turns blue every two minutes in your classroom you can't dish out final-tier punishments for every offence – if you begin with 'okay, that's a detention!', you are limiting your options for a follow-up (as well as risking having an entire class in detention!).

I once took a post in a residential EBD and was stunned at the liberal attitude some staff had towards swearing in Y10 and Y11 groups. I had worked in very strict EBD settings prior to that and I decided that despite most of staffs' liberal attitude to foul language, I wasn't having it. It took me a few weeks but eventually there was no swearing in my class.

This is how I did it: by being totally consistent (making sure every incidence of swearing was addressed) and by making time to build up strong relationships with the boys in the group. I spent time with them after lessons - played football and other games with them at break, helped them with their work at lunch time and after school, went out on evening trips etc. I know what you're thinking and yes, it did involve a lot of extra work for me but the results justified it. It meant I only had to say "Oi, pack the language in" and they would comply – they respected me because they knew I cared about them. Eventually it ceased to be a problem at all - and these kids were the roughest of the rough!

Other strategies to manage swearing:

1. Host a discussion session. Give students an opportunity to discuss the issue of swearing and set their own ground rules. Let them discuss what they would or would not find acceptable, and what they would do about "offenders". Discuss with the class how you convey respect. How you speak conveys respect or disrespect, care or disdain etc. What message is it sending when we use foul language? How should we speak and why? What impression would others have of us if we used foul language in public – for example in a restaurant with our girlfriend/boyfriend? Is that how we want to be viewed? What would be the advantages/disadvantages of being viewed negatively by others?

2. Refuse to be drawn in. Students will say "Oh but we use this kind of language all the time." "My Mum and Dad say that" etc.

Your response:

"Maybe so but we do not speak like that in this class. I don't use that kind of language with you. I don't expect you to use that kind of language here in this classroom. Okay? Thank you".

3. Don't make a big deal about it Remember this student is probably trying to provoke a reaction. Rather than show your disgust, first ensure the other students are occupied then take the offender aside calmly and deal with them out of earshot of the rest of the class.

4. Set up a 'swear box'. You can't take their money but you can hit them where it hurts by depriving them of merits, time, computer use etc. For each offence put a token of your own invention in the box (or chart), with sanctions taking effect when the pre-arranged threshold is reached.

5. Engage support from parents. Try to encourage parents/ guardians to follow up at home by encouraging polite language and discouraging swearing. You could suggest that 'The Sopranos' probably isn't the kind of family drama they should be watching () but probably better to just explain that the incidents of inappropriate language are a problem in lessons and will become more of a problem for the student in future if they aren't checked.

How to get students to follow your instructions

Have you ever asked students to get on with their work only to turn round five minutes later and see that they've totally ignored your instructions? (And if you say no, I don't believe you!). Then, when you ask them why they aren't doing as you asked do they just say *"I didn't hear you"* or *"I didn't know what you meant."*

This is a very effective excuse for them because it puts the onus straight back on the teacher - you. After all, if they didn't hear your instructions or didn't understand them, it can only be your fault for not being clear enough.

Your only course of action in this situation (without seeming like an unfair bully) is to give them the benefit of the doubt and a second chance. As I said, it's an effective excuse because it legitimately grants them a considerable amount of time off task.

The reason students give excuses instead of following instructions is often simply because they can. If your instructions aren't clearly understood you give them a reason to argue, complain and not do as you ask.

Don't worry though, I have a cunning plan for you to use in these situations. Here it is...

1: Make sure you have their full attention before giving instructions. Make sure they are looking at you and not fiddling with a pencil, turning around, looking at a book, etc. One quite ingenious way of getting eye contact is to hold your pen up in front of you and then move it slowly so that it is in front of your face. The pen will attract the student's gaze and they will then follow it until their eyes are in line with yours. It works - like magic!

2: Be congruent. Congruence is the process of making sure that the silent messages we give through our facial expressions, body language, voice tone, pitch and volume clearly match the actual words we use. When you're being congruent, all aspects of communication are in sync. In short, we clearly mean what we say.

Our students will read everything about our approach, our gestures and the way we look at them before we actually start to speak and if we get any of these crucial aspects wrong they will have decided to listen, switch off or retaliate before we even open our mouths. It is the silent messages we unconsciously give that are often at the root of students' decisions to behave as they do.

Are we giving them the message that we are tired and worn out? If we do there's a good chance they'll either ignore us or push a little harder to tip us over the edge when we ask them to do something they'd rather not.

Are we giving them the message that we're angry with them? If so they might well turn against us completely. Tougher students might retaliate there and then while the more timid ones might hold a grudge and seek retribution at a later date. In either case, they are unlikely to behave as we would like and at best we will get reluctant compliance.

The way we give instructions has a massive impact on how students respond to them. We can give the impression that we are a pushover, a threat or a leader depending on the silent messages we give out. Use assertive body language – claim your space in the classroom, adopt an open stance, use a calm, measured speaking voice and avoid frowning, scowling or pointing.

3: Make sure your instructions are clear and unambiguous.
Students need to be told exactly and specifically what you want them to do.

"John, you need to stop tapping your pen, stop swinging on your chair and look this way."

...will have more chance of getting the desired outcome than:

"John, stop it!"

A request like this leaves us open to questions...

"Stop what, miss?"

...and then before we know it, we're into an argument.

Vague terms like 'quietly', 'properly', 'sensibly' and 'respectfully' cause problems in the classroom. Straight away they open the door to confrontation...

For example:

"Get on with your work quietly please."

For one student 'quietly' means 'whispering' while for another it means talking in their normal speaking voice. Another student might take this as meaning there is no real rule on noise levels at all. And what you probably meant was 'work in silence'!

In each case, a student who is challenged for making too much noise or swinging on their chair will almost certainly protest that they are "working quietly" or "sitting properly". It's not surprising that vague instructions like this don't always result in the behaviour we want to see and are often a source of arguments. Wherever there are ambiguous instructions there will be a student breaking the rules.

To make sure the students keep within the noise levels or sit appropriately we want we would need to clarify what we mean by 'quietly' or 'properly'. Younger children might need a tangible representation of the word - they could be shown a ruler and told to use their '30cm voices' or their 'partner voices' instead of their 'yard voices' (yard being the big concrete thing they play in, not the imperial measurement). For older students we might simply clarify our instruction by demonstrating the volume we are referring to.

To get a student to stop swinging on a chair more explicit instructions are required:

"John, sit on your chair like everyone else so that all four chair legs are on the floor."

It may sound pedantic but it avoids opportunities for the *'I am sitting properly'* arguments.

4: Smile. It takes the sting out of your instructions for students who rebel against authority and it shows you are confident.

5: Ask them to confirm that they heard the instructions. This is the key step because once they've told you, they can't ever come back at you with "I didn't understand" or "I didn't hear you".

"Darren, what did I just ask you to do?"

"Kyle, tell me what I just said please."

"John, repeat the instructions please so I know you heard me."

Other classroom management strategies to get students to follow your instructions:

i) Give them a reason. In 1978 a group of research psychologists investigating human behaviour tried to determine the factors which make people more likely to do favours for others. They set up an experiment involving a photocopier machine and tried three different approaches to get people to let them jump the queue:

1. **Request only:** "Excuse me, do you mind if I go before you to use the photocopier?"

2. **'Made up' or irrelevant reason:** "Excuse me, do you mind if I go before you to use the photocopier because I have to make some copies?"

3. **Real reason:** "Excuse me, do you mind if I go before you to use the photocopier because I'm in a terrible rush?"

So a third of the time they just asked to skip the line, a third of the time they gave an irrelevant reason (of course they were there to make copies!), and a third of the time they actually gave a good reason ('I'm in a hurry').

The research yielded interesting results. When the researchers gave a reason for wanting to queue-jump they were allowed to do so far more than when simply making the request without a reason. The most surprising part of the study was that it didn't seem to matter what the reason was - a totally irrelevant reason ('Can I go first? I really like the 2012 Olympic logo') worked just as well as a legitimate one.

The point we can take from this study in relation to our classroom management strategies is that when making a request for a student to do something, we should back up it up with a reason: "Can you do this please... and this is why it would be a good idea").

It doesn't necessarily have to be a good reason...

"Get on with your work because otherwise you won't get it finished" should work just as well as "Get on with your work otherwise you'll have to finish it at break"; and will undoubtedly stimulate fewer arguments and protests.

Try:

"Help me by quietening down please, I have a hangover headache" ... *rather than snapping "Be quiet!"*

"Line up please, because we're running out of time." ...rather than "Line up please."

Giving them a reason for doing something also means you can attach importance to the instructions without coming across as officious and bureaucratic:

"When you come to see me at lunch time get here for 12:30 so we can sort this out without it interfering with your lunch too much." ...rather than "See me at lunch time, without fail."

Play around with it and see what happens... but don't get carried away or you might get in trouble ("give me your dinner money because I'm badly paid" will almost certainly make you unpopular on yard duty).

ii) Closed requests. Starting a request with 'thank you' before they've done what you're asking them to, gives the clear impression that we expect them to respond positively. We all know the effect of positive expectations so it comes as no surprise that requests phrased in this way tend to give favourable results, often having a quite magical effect on students.

"Thank you for lining up straight away."

Sometimes people don't pay attention to the information they are receiving; only the structure of phrasings and sentences. If you can fit your request inside a structure that people are used to complying with, there's a good chance that they'll comply. By following up with some quiet 1:1 praise we can cement the fact that the student has successfully followed instructions.

"Thank you for doing as I asked – it makes my job much easier."

How to deal with silly behaviour

Here's a classroom management strategy for dealing with silly students – the ones that disrupt lessons with immature, attention-seeking behaviour.

I've often found that those students who 'need' to show off and crave attention benefit from being given the opportunity to do exactly that – albeit in a controlled way. Please understand that this classroom management strategy is not about condoning or encouraging inappropriate 'calling out' from students but if a kid has a tremendous sense of humour it should be (sensibly) encouraged as long as you can do so without losing your control, and without creating a disorderly atmosphere of 'anything goes'.

Consider these two different approaches:

Example # 1:

Teacher: *"Jonny, I'm fed up of you messing about! If it happens again you're in detention."*

(Jonny carries on behaving like an idiot to gain approval from his peers).

Teacher: *"Right Jonny, that's it, I warned you, you're in detention."*

Example #2:

Teacher calls Jonny outside class before the lesson starts.

Teacher: *"Hey Jonny can I have a quick word? Listen, you've got an incredible talent. Do you know what it is?"*

Student: *"Um..."*

Teacher: *"You've got an incredible talent for making people laugh - you're very lucky. It's a very worthwhile skill and will make you very popular. But we've got a bit of a problem. When you do it in the middle of the lesson or when I'm trying to get the class to work it distracts everyone because they all fall about laughing (teacher smiles). Right?"*

Student: *"Er, yeah."*

Teacher: *"So how about this ... I give you a set time for your comedy routines and cabaret but the rest of the time you keep quiet. How would that suit you?"*

Student: *"What do you mean?"*

Teacher: *"I'll give you five minutes somewhere in the lesson – either at the beginning, the end or somewhere in the middle if we need a* *break and you can tell some of your jokes. But there are a couple of rules: the jokes have to be clean and non-racist; you can only start when I give you the signal; you have to stop when I give you the signal. If you can't do that then we'll have to go back to the detention thing and I don't think either of us really want that. Ok?"*

Hopefully you can see from the two examples that the attitude of the teacher when dealing with challenging and attention-seeking kids is crucial. It can make a small problem much worse - or it can turn it into a learning opportunity.

[Questions from the Real World]

Julia Thompson & Rob Plevin

Question: How can you get more lively students interested in the lesson? I give them more work and they get too silly.

Julia Thompson: First of all when we have very lively students there is a noise control issue and what you need to do is actually teach kids how to play games and how to play quietly – you have to teach kids to practice games before you actually play a game.

So if you have trouble with the game then you have ways to manage it. Have short games so that it doesn't get too silly, play just a couple of short games so that they don't have time to get silly and so that they get to practice being quiet and sensible when asked to do so.

Sometimes teachers find it hard to manage large groups – so put them in pairs to play together, there are all kinds of little short activities they can do, it should be interesting to review but if they work in pairs the kids can sometimes get too silly so large groups might not work – I would never go above 3 to start with. The pairs tend to work well together – you might get kids interested to work together – if they are lively and if they are noisy teach them how to control that noise and keep them in small groups.

Also, if you want to get students interested in a lesson, use the technology that you have. There are thousands of online sites of pictures to play games and I would like to recommend one that can used by almost anybody who can read and that is the web site www.freerice.com this is an amazing site that will engage students for hours, it is highly addictive.

Graduate students can play it, or strangers can play it and major English learners can play it – pick a word in the vocabulary for example and you have four choices for an answer when you click on the right one, ten grains of rice are donated to the world food programme so it brings out the best in students. These students are extremely poor and wherever you play this game you do good in the world. So we get them involved in individual games and they are busy and lively and they are doing something for someone else, it brings out the best in them.

Rob Plevin: OK I am going to give you a quick story which kind of links up with this. I was covering a colleague's lesson delivering a science lesson to a group of students (14 year olds) who had been banned by their usual teacher from doing practical work.

Innocently, not knowing this had happened, I said, "we're going to be using chemicals today" and they said, "No, no, no - we don't do practical work, we are not allowed to use the equipment!" I couldn't believe it – the teacher had decided that they were too silly to be doing anything active – they were only allowed to work from worksheets every single lesson. I mean, now and again I can understand a group being told they won't be allowed to do practical work for a day or two – because of poor behaviour in a previous lesson – but to ban them forever is just crazy! No wonder they were known as a bad group – they were bored stiff!!

"Listen, I think we should start afresh," I said. "I think we should start again and I am going to trust you that you can actually behave responsibly enough to use the equipment and do a practical session."

The look on their faces was a picture. They couldn't believe that this was happening – but I added "there is a proviso...", and I very carefully explained what would happen if they couldn't keep it together. I said "we are just going to try it for ten minutes just to start with and if you're doing well we'll carry on. It's up to you guys to show me that you can be trusted. Does that sound fair?"

They worked so hard you know – they were so grateful that they had been given a chance. They were one of my favourite groups after that. We had a lot of fun.

I think breaking things down into small chunks sometimes works, some kids just can't handle the big picture, it needs to be broken down and you need to keep giving them reminders along the way. You need to very clearly explain what will happen if the game goes wrong – if it doesn't work, if they get too daft – and you obviously have to have some backup work up your sleeve ready for when that happens.

So basically I would be a little bit more prepared about how you approach this and start small with them, give them a chance and show them that you trust them – so maybe just have a conversation with them to start off with and say "look things haven't been working but I want you to have fun so we are going to start again and here is how it is going to work. We are going to start off with this small activity and see if we can build on that."

The disruptive joker

The joker is desperate for attention. His smart remarks, rude comments, smutty gestures, witty retorts and wisecracks may be funny (unfortunately, some class comedians really are!) but they are often a smokescreen to mask frustration, disappointment, low self-esteem and inability to fit in. Here are some suggestions...

1. Make sure he knows the extent of the problem. Often this child won't be aware of the problem he is causing; he thinks everything is okay because he's getting a few laughs. Having it explained in private that he is actually starting to annoy the majority of his peers can have a dramatic effect on him – because this is the opposite of his desired effect. Impress upon him that he may well be turning students against himself by acting in this way and that you don't want to see that happening. Tell them you have a nifty set of consequences which you will implement with the sole intention of helping him kick his silly and disruptive habit.

2. Explain consequences clearly. Make sure he knows exactly what will happen if he continues disrupting the lesson. Be sure to tell him this is not a personal vendetta against him – it's the only way you know to help him remember how to behave in lessons and succeed.

3. Try not to show emotion when reprimanding him. Because of the dire craving for attention the last thing you want to do is reward the joker with an outburst, regardless of how many of your buttons he has pressed. Instead, issue consequences calmly and without any fuss at all – every time he acts inappropriately. Don't give in to his protests either – just take the wind out of his sails with the following lines:

"I've told you what is happening, you made your choice. If you want to talk more about this we can do it later; come and see me after school, I'll be in my room. Now get on with your work."

...and then turn your back, click your heels and march off into the sunset. Or back to your desk, whichever is nearer.

4. Remember the positive alternative. This student is desperate for attention so you should be ready and eager to pay some out – but only when he does something right. Praise is a very effective management strategy and you should lump as much attention as you can possibly muster when he is settled and working – throw confetti, bring in a brass band, jump on the table and shout with joy... but only when he has deserved it.

If you can stick to the 'no attention and no-fuss consequence' for inappropriate behaviour and 'immediate sincere attention' for the right behaviour you can see miracles occur surprisingly quickly.

Dealing with angry, defiant students

Here are some classroom management strategies for dealing with angry, defiant students.

1. Remain detached and calm. Defiant behaviour is often a cry for help or an attempt to cover a fear of failure. Nobody wants to look stupid in front of others (except those in the audition stages of the X-Factor) and arguing against authority can be an effective distraction and a way of avoiding looking foolish. Being sensitive to your students' needs and the reasons behind their behaviour, rather than assuming they are being belligerent, makes it less likely you will do or say something that will only aggravate the situation and make matters worse. Remember also that their behaviour is most probably not aimed at you so try not to appear to take it personally.

2. Offer help or support. Offering support is a very positive and totally non-confrontational first response and is therefore one of the best ways to deal with a student who is digging themselves into a deep hole. It also strengthens the staff/student relationship.

'I can see you've made a start but do you need me to explain that bit again for you? Would it help if I let you start on one of the other questions first?'

'Do you need to get a drink or some fresh air?'

'I can see you're getting angry about this, why don't you go and sit over there quietly for a few minutes and then let me know when you need some help?'

'Is there anything I can do that will make this easier for you?'

3. Ask for their help or advice. Asking students for help catches them completely off guard, immediately changes their negative state and can, more than any other technique I've tried, disarm the angriest of teenagers and get them on side.

I think we all, on some deep level, like to feel 'needed' and this is the easiest way of tapping into this primitive human trait.

"John I know you're very good with technical equipment – can you help me set up the AV suite please? We can talk about your homework after that."

"Simon I've got a bit of a problem. My son is really struggling with one of his teachers at school. You remind me of him and I'm impressed with the way you have managed to turn yourself around over the last few months. Can you give me some advice to pass on to him?"

"Tony I could do with your help here. I don't want to be on your case all the time – what do you suggest we do?"

3. Give them a classroom responsibility. Our most challenging students often have leadership qualities (the ring leaders) and are in desperate need of attention. Meet this need on your terms by giving them a responsibility. This can have remarkable (and very fast) results.

Try putting them in charge of equipment or giving them a job such as an errand or keeping other students settled.

4. Remove audience pressure. Some students will try to escalate the incident in front of peers. If possible speak to the student privately or redirect them so as to deal with the problem later.

"Let's not talk about it here – it could be embarrassing for both of us. Come and see me at lunch time so that you can tell me everything that's bothering you – and come early so that you still get your break."

5. De-escalate, deflect and defuse. Any form of distraction such as asking them an off-topic questions or diverting them towards a new activity/scene can switch their attention, take the heat out of a situation and provide the necessary change in state.

Quite innocently I once responded to a very irate, tantrum-throwing teenage boy with the question 'what colour are your socks?' His change in state was immediate and the expression on his face changed from wild-eyed fury to utter bewilderment in a trice as he stood, puzzled, looking at me. His mood was transformed and we both fell about laughing. 'What colour are your socks?' (or an equally random question) is now my standard response to anyone displaying a hissy-fit.

Another de-escalation strategy is simply not to react; say nothing and just look at them. Ignore their socks altogether.

Silence is very powerful at times like this. The student wants a response and by meeting them with an impassive look and total silence you clearly convey that you are on total control and will not be drawn into an argument. One of the greatest ways to deal with someone who wants an argument and get them to stop and think and reflect on their behaviour is to deny them a reaction of any kind.

6. Give them opportunity to succeed. Tasks pitched to their interests and ability level give them the opportunity to experience success and raise their self esteem. If fear of failing at a task in front of peers is driving their negative behaviour they need sufficient opportunity to succeed and experience 'a-ha!' moments to improve their attitude. It's difficult to feel fed up when you feel a sense of success and achievement.

7. Acknowledge any improvement in attitude. It's easy to continually focus on negative behaviour when dealing with particularly challenging students but the quickest way to make lasting positive changes to their behaviour is always with positive comments. When was the last time you did something to please someone who was constantly nagging you?

If they make a slight improvement be quick to jump on it and 'catch them being good'. Tell them specifically what they have done and why you are so pleased with them.

8. Encourage and facilitate cooperative group work. Positive relationships between peers (and staff) need to be established and continually developed if students' negative attitudes towards school/ college are to be addressed. All students (particularly those who are opting out) need to be made to feel welcome and part of the classroom community. Peer relationships can be strengthened through regular team building activities and cooperative group work.

9. Go through stepped consequences as per school behaviour policy.

For example:

- move them to an isolated seat

- take time off them at break/after school

- notify them of a letter/phone call home

- 'park' them in another class

- send them to senior staff

When moving through consequences give a fair warning to remind them of the consequences of their actions if they continue. And try to give them 'take up time' to follow your instructions rather than standing over them expecting immediate compliance. With audience pressure, that's a tall order.

"Chris this is the third and final time I'm going to ask you to sit down. You've had your warnings and you know what happens next. It's your choice."

"John if you don't make a start now you'll be... (insert consequence of choice). Is that really what you want? I'm going to go and help John and I'll be back over in 2 minutes. I'll expect to see that you've completed that first question by the time I return; if you don't you'll be back in at break. It's your choice."

[Questions from the Real World]

Andy Vass

Question: How can I control tough students?

Andy Vass: One thing that gets in the way of effective teaching is trying to control students and children – you can't, there isn't a teacher I know who can control kids.

What we have got to do is to just say "No". Even when they get taken out of class, even when they get to the senior staff, even when they get sent to the principal, even when they get sent home we haven't controlled them and we haven't won - it is not a contest.

The only thing that we can control (as explained by Rob earlier) is us, ourselves. I don't know whether or not you have come across a book called "The seven habits of highly effective people" by Steven Covey – he has got a little equation in there which I often refer to it's called E + R = O. The Event plus your choice of Response determines the Outcome, and it's that response – now I am using the word Response not React.

Respond means to be calm, measured, confident – think about response rather than react. It conveys calmness, professionalism, thought, cognition. So control equals confidence. Control your inner dialogue, control your psychology, control your behaviours it certainly equals confidence. But for heaven's sake don't try and control kids because you will use up a lot of energy and fail miserably.

[Questions from the Real World]

Tom McIntyre

Question: When an assignment is challenging, she folds her arms stamps her feet & refuses to do any work. When I divide the class into groups she tells me who she will work with. She really dominates and the other students follow her lead.

The ABA (applied behavior analysis) folks and their A-B-C analysis would say that the purpose of her behavior is to escape something she dislikes (negative reinforcement). The PsychoEducational folks & Driekurs "Mistaken Goals analysis" would say that she is on the border of the Attention-seeking & Power seeking stages (find more on these assessments and their meaning at BehaviorAdvisor.com (inside the "Intervention Strategies" button, click on "Figuring out why kids misbehave").

While I recognize the validity of the A-B-C assessment, it only serves to identify "surface" factors that influence behavior. The ABAers don't venture inside the skull. I'm inclined to think that the behavior is intended to keep contact with you... the desire to "belong" to you (Driekurs' model). With that approach in mind, I'd recommend setting up system to have her earn time with you. Additionally teach alternative behaviors to obtain what she wants & prompt them, or recognize those actions when she shows them. You'll find strategies for teaching those better behaviors at BehaviorAdvisor.com (inside the "Intervention Strategies" section, on the "social skills" page)

Be sure that you avoid praise that focuses on the score attained on a test/assignment, and shift it to a style of recognition that addresses effort expended and progress made. The reasons can be found at BehaviorAdvisor.com (click on Intervention Strategies, and scroll down to the web page on praise).

While you're inside the Intervention Strategies part of BehaviorAdvisor.com, check out the page on the "Problem solving meeting". It's a way to use conversation to spur change for the better.

Dealing with an extremely difficult group

Here are a few classroom management strategies to help when working with a very challenging group of students.

1. Divide and conquer. Split the group according to your seating plan. Tell them that if they want to sit with their friends they have to earn that privilege. Use a calendar to show the number of lessons there are left this year and tell them that as long as they work quietly and respectfully, you will change the seating plan after another ten lessons. That way, as long as they behave appropriately, they will be able to enjoy the majority of the year's lessons sitting with their friends.

2. Use LOTS of warranted, genuine praise. Be quick to thank and acknowledge students in this group when they do the right thing.

You may have to test the best way to do this. Some students, who are lucky to part of a generally supportive class, may be grateful for public praise while in some groups receiving praise from the teacher can result in students being ridiculed for being 'goody-two-shoes'. Try private praise outside the room (after/before the lesson) and written praise – postcards/letters home. When negative behaviour has become entrenched (as it does with a very difficult group), focusing on what the students are doing RIGHT is the best way to turn the tide.

3. Insist on a short period of silent work in each lesson. Offer a number of choices of work of varying difficulty and let the students choose what they want but... insist they do the work they have chosen in silence. Insisting on short periods (up to ten minutes) of silent work gives students (and you) a break from constant noise and reminds them that YOU are in charge.

4. Don't raise your voice to be heard. Any teacher who struggles to be heard over classroom noise will be perceived to be weak, and ignored by students. Always wait until they are totally silent before speaking to them en masse, use a quiet speaking voice (if anything you should speak with less volume than usual to make them have to try harder to hear you) and limit the number of times you stop them or interrupt them to give instructions. If you have a lot of directions to give, do so quietly by addressing small groups and individuals rather than the whole group.

5. Stay positive. There is a tendency, understandable when faced with a disruptive class, to stop trying hard to engage them and instead allow yourself to be backed into punishing them with dull, uninspiring lesson tasks and negative classroom management strategies. The occasional 'copying from the board' or 'worksheet-based' lesson is fine to remind them what they're missing, or to give yourself a well-earned break, but if these tedious activities become the norm, behaviour will undoubtedly deteriorate. Believe in the value of good education and let the students see that you want them to succeed. Ask them the type of activities they would like to do in the lesson and strive to include as many of their suggestions as is realistically possible. In time they will respect you for this.

[Questions from the Real World]

Tom McIntyre

Question: I'm teaching Pre-K4 & short attention span is part of the problem. Can you suggest quick technique can use to get & hold attention?

Use a whisper voice to say: *"Anyone who can hear me, raise your hand."*

Lower the volume more (rather than yell) to get attention. As the kids find you

harder to hear, they shoosh each other.

Acting is a large part of drawing the attention of students. Be dramatic in voice & actions.

Interact with your assistant teacher. That give-and-take helps to keep attention.

Ask questions of kids:

"I'm going to ask someone a question on this in the next 2 minutes. Who will it be? We'll see. Listen closely." (Notice the cadence & rhyme of the utterance).

"Who can show me how we walk back to our desks?" "Who can show me

how we sit like pretzels on the rug?" Complement those who do well.

Praise youngsters for correct behavior in an attempt to engage the "ripple effect":

Use "Auctioneering" praise – or behavioural narration. Say: "I see 3 kids who are ready. Can I get 5? Yes! Can I see 10 of my students doing...."

Have a chant to return their attention to you:

Say "I-2-3, eyes on me." They say in return, "1-2, eyes on you."

Practice it with them to make it a routine.

[Questions from the Real World]

Angela Watson

Question: We have a lot of students with pretty severe behaviour issues at my school; do you hold the same expectations for behaviour for them? What if they aren't successful and the other students see it as them as always getting away with unacceptable behaviour?

Angela: You know what I do in this situation - it's a little bit unconventional. There are a handful of kids in every class that are extremely challenging, and if you are lucky it's only two or three. What we as teachers tend to do is we pretend that they are not challenging in front of the other students because we want to project a calm image and that's good. The other kids in the classroom aren't dumb, they know who the troublemakers are, they know what their issues are, they are well aware of what's happening. One year I had a student who would get extremely violent in class, he would throw desks at students, and act in ways that were extremely inappropriate and I realised that it was time to stop pretending that things like that weren't happening and just kind of smoothing everything over and really involve the whole class in a discussion about it.

The result of that I thought was so good that I started doing it even with less severe behaviours. So after the student calmed down (I'll call him Kevin) I said to the class, "You all noticed that Kevin has problems controlling his anger sometimes – have you ever felt that way? What did you do about it?" And we talked about appropriate and inappropriate responses to feelings of anger and then I asked, "What can we do as a class to help Kevin manage his anger?" and I wrote that down.

Now I had been doing all those things I have shared with you on the webinar to build a classroom community and a supportive learning environment, so the kids were used to problem solving like this as a class. Kevin wasn't the least bit embarrassed about it because he heard me bring all kinds of issues to the class and he knew the conversation was going to be really kind and supportive of him, and before that conversation I felt like I was working all by myself to handle this kid my school wasn't doing enough to support me and I was trying to shelter and protect the rest of the class from him, but from that moment on I felt that we were all on the same page and that other students were working together to help this child.

If Kevin got angry he would rip down a bulletin board and I knew that the best thing was not to confront him at that moment, I no longer felt pressure to respond. The other kids stopped looking at me as though they were saying, "What are you going to do about this, is he going to get away with it?" Instead they started looking at me and at him really sympathetically. They tried to comfort him and they tried to calm him down using the techniques that we talked about and I could just level with him and say, "Guys, Kevin says he needs space to just breathe and calm down as he is so angry – remember? So just back up and leave him alone right now and I'll talk with him later about his choices."

So the answer to your question is yes, just hold those kids with severe behaviour issues to the same standard as everyone else in the sense that you want them to aspire to those behaviours but you don't have to rush in and punish them or confront them every time they fall short if that's not going to help them improve. Focus on building up a sense of your classroom community instead and have everyone work together and encourage the child along the way that's improvement for me. And if someone questions why you are letting the child get away with unacceptable behaviours I say, "She's not making a good choice right now. Self-control is hard for all of us sometimes and that's something she's working on, you should be really proud about how well your doing in that area and the good choices you are making right now so we are going to work together as a class to help everyone get better and better with self-control."

Students who lack self esteem

[Questions from the Real World]

Andy Vass

Question: How do you motivate students who have stepped out of discouraged home environment? How do you undo the damage being done to get the self-esteem at home?

Andy Vass: It's very sad isn't it and very tough, we are part of a caring profession, we always want to make a difference to kids' lives but when I read that question a couple of things popped into my mind. One was the story of the starfish you know the one, where there are thousands of starfish washed up on the beach and there's a person walking along and they're throwing them back into the sea as fast as they can and somebody says, "what are you wasting your energy for, there are thousands of them they are going to die, you are not making a difference" and they say, "well I am to these ones."

It's important to make the difference we can make rather than the difference we would like to make but can't. What about Mother Theresa? People said "why do you give these people a bed when they are going to be dead in a few hours?" and her reply was, "just so that one point in their life they know that somebody cares" and I think that's what we have to get across.

So when I see these students I tell them things about them, not their behaviour, about them being a person. "I look at you and see somebody who is smart, I see somebody who is kind, I see somebody who shares, I see somebody who can make friends" – whatever. It has to be true, of course. I remember working with a girl that I was told was incredibly stubborn and I treated her as if she was determined.

That is how we frame some of the things, some of our beliefs and even prejudices about kids matter. There is something else and I can't go into it in massive detail because time precludes – use feedback rather than praise. Kids with low self-esteem do not believe you when you praise them and remember we only feel good when we have done something to feel good. So emphasise the 'doing' - "When I saw you inviting Michelle to play that game with you, that tells me you're the kind of person who is really kind and thoughtful." Again focus on the doing. "You've got your date, you've got your title, you've begun to draw in pencil – I imagine you are pleased with that." Keep the descriptive feedback rather than the praise and judgment because kids with low self-esteem don't believe you.

Arguments and serious incidents

Here are eight quick ways to de-escalate arguments and serious incidents.

1. Avoid asking 'Why?'. Here's something you should avoid when confronting students about their behaviour or attitude – using the word 'why'. Asking a student why they have or haven't done something is an extremely confrontational and threatening way of approaching and almost always results in more conflict. Asking why puts them on the defensive: "Why are you sitting like that?", "Why do you have to behave like this?", "Why won't you listen?"

Can you see how these questions can lead to more arguments and increased conflict? If you don't believe this is true just try putting the same questions to your partner tonight - but have the spare room ready!

A better alternative is to ask 'how' or 'what' questions, to give people the opportunity to explain themselves without making them feel they are being accused of something. "What makes you want to do that?", "What were you thinking to end up doing that?", "How can you make sure this doesn't happen in future?", "How could you do it better?"

2. Create a diversion.

A diversion can be:

- a change in activity (always have a game up your sleeve)

- redirection of attention to a demonstration or something else happening nearby ("come and have a look at this over here")

- a story or joke ("Hey I heard you were picked for the football team this week... Why don't you tell me more about it?")

- a fight between two prisoners to keep the German guards occupied

I discovered, quite by accident, the power of diversions when working with a group of 15 year old boys who had been excluded from mainstream school. I had taken them for a game of football in a public park and a fight broke out between two of them. I separated them and took Andrew, who was extremely wound up, to the side line and tried to calm him down. He was completely out of control, wailing, screaming and hurling abuse at the other boy and nothing I said or did seemed to have an effect on him. He was completely hysterical.

Embarrassed at how bad this situation looked with members of the public sitting and walking nearby, I looked at the ground to gather my thoughts. Andrew's day-glo socks suddenly caught my attention and I was surprised to hear myself say to him...

"Wow Andy, what colour are your socks?"

It was a completely off-topic question and was obviously a surprise to him too. As if by magic he immediately fell silent and glanced down at his feet before looking up at me with a quizzical expression on his face. The screaming and swearing had stopped and he stood perfectly still. I looked back him and for a few seconds we stood staring at each other before falling about laughing.

All my efforts to calm him down using the usual methods had failed. I tried giving him warnings and I tried giving him consequences. I tried being more supportive and I tried cajoling him. But when a person is lost in frenzy those things don't work. What did work in this instance (and I think it's an excellent all-round de-escalation strategy) was to radically and quickly alter the student's mental state so as to interrupt their thought pattern and stop them from being 'stuck' in hysteria. Any off-topic question should do the job or, if you're more adventurous, you could change your behaviour and do something they aren't expecting. Try not to punch them though.

3. Remind them of past successes

"Think back to yesterday, do you remember how the conversation we had and how you behaved?"

"Remember how well you coped last time this happened?"

"Hey, I saw you behaving impeccably this morning. Come on, get back to your true self."

4. Silence. Just look at them. Let them rant and rave, the storm will eventually blow itself out. Then ask:

"What was behind all that? What's the matter?"

You might be very surprised at how open a student will be with you when you refuse to be their enemy and instead just 'listen'. Selective silence is one of the most effective ways of dealing with difficult people. It is easy to use, and very low threat. When people are being difficult, they are often seeking attention and power. When you respond verbally to an attack you are giving them attention and power they desire. When you use selective silence you deny them both attention and power.

5. Offer Support.

"What do you want me to do to help you?"

"How can we sort this out?"

6. Use humour.

"Calm down. Hold your breath until you turn bright purple and then we'll talk about this."

7. Offer them space.

"I don't want you to leave but I also don't want things to get out of control so how about this? If you need to leave the room and compose

yourself I understand – there's the door, you can come back when you're ready and there are no hard feelings."

8. Deny them an enemy – agree with them or apologise.

"I think you're right. I'm going to work on that, you've made me think that maybe I am a little bit too bossy sometimes. Will you accept my apology so we can start again?"

"Neither of us really wants this to escalate so I'm going to leave it there. We can talk about it later if you want."

9. Partially agree with them:

You can deflect confrontation with students by acknowledging their concerns or partially agreeing with them. It goes like this...

"I agree it may not seem fair but. ..."

"That may be true but you're still going to have to..."

So let's say a teacher tells a child to stop talking. The student might deny that they were talking. The teacher then insists they saw them talking. They bat "Yes you were"/"no I wasn't" back and forth for a while. Then the student appeals to those around him for witnesses and complains about always being picked on. By now the class have stopped working and are enjoying the show. The whole thing escalates way out of proportion to the original incident. Here's a better script using the 'partial agreement strategy:

Teacher: *Fred, you need to stop talking.*

Fred: *I wasn't even talking.*

Teacher: *You may be right. You just need to finish exercise three.*

There is nothing to fight against if you have just been agreed with. So, the student has the opportunity to make things right and without loss of face.

[Questions from the Real World]

LouAnne Johnson

Question: Do you have any experiences of dealing with threats of violence and if so how?

LouAnne Johnson: I once had a student that offered to kill another teacher because he heard that teacher shouting at me one day, and he said it would cost $250. I said thanks for the offer but I think I will pass it up this time.

I think it's important to be aware and to accept that society is dangerous, the whole world is dangerous today there is no safe place so you have to accept that. But if you are literally frightened of your students probably because of their skin colour then it's your problem and I think you need to deal with it because students are like puppies, they can sense fear and that makes them think they are the alpha dog plus you can't teach them when you feel like that – you just can't, it's not going to happen.

So if you have fears that are created by the media or based on ignorance or not being exposed to someone then that's your problem. If you do have really scary students and you feel scared of them then I say you need to find another population to work with so that you are not afraid of your students.

I forgot to tell you that I had a kid that came up to me one time when there was no-one there and I was sitting in my room. He was a big kid. He was wearing a tank top which they weren't supposed to do but he wanted me to see how big his muscles were and they were giant and he came up and he said, "You know I could hurt you" and I said, "Yeah you could hurt me but I tell you what I'll give you one free hit and then I am going to kill you" he just looked at me and I said, "Just before you hit me what about this, you might be younger and stronger than I am but I am older and meaner than you are and I am going to hurt you because I am an old lady and I am going to kick your butt and if I do everyone is going to laugh at you forever. " And he just stood there and then I said, "Wait, wait, wait! before you hit me think about this if you get rid of me who is going to take my place, who do you think is going to love you the way I do because you know if I didn't love you I wouldn't be here" and I just kept doing that so finally he just rolled his eyes and said, "You're crazy" and I said, "I know I agree I have brain damage but you can be a teacher even if you have brain damage."

He just replied, "Never mind," so he left and I went to talk to one of our security guards who teaches Kung Fu and I asked him if he would help me, so we did a little display out on the lawn one day and I put him down on the ground – he put me in a neck lock and I put him down and I asked him not to tell them that he let me and he agreed. When the kids went over and asked him he said, "Don't mess with her she's tough!" I like to use humour if you can because you can't hate someone who makes you laugh.

[Questions from the Real World]

LouAnne Johnson

Question: I don't want to believe it but sometimes you just have to accept that some kids are impossible to reach given time and resources do you agree?

LouAnne: I have coupled that with another one which was similar, talking about a student who didn't care and when the teacher went to talk to the parent, the father said that he didn't care either so she asked what she could do. Obviously you can't do anything about parents they have had their own negative experiences about school, what you can try to do is create a positive engaging experience for the student but it doesn't happen immediately.

This is a really hard thing to accept but it's necessary because when you can spend 95% of our energy on the 5% of the students who are really, really difficult to reach and that then leaves the 90% that are somewhat interested and then you always have that core students who really do want to learn. I think they get the raw end of the deal a lot of the time because we are spending so much energy trying to catch those students who are slipping away.

For every person it's an individual personal decision but I spent (when I first started teaching) far too much energy going after students who didn't want to learn and what I learned was watching a guy called Craig Camon who was a horse trainer, he said that if you chase after a horse, the more you chase it the more it will run. If you are trying to do something new what you do is you offer something interesting – a chance to stand still the horse will come to you. So I tried to do the same thing with the students, I would offer something interesting but not chase them around and try to force them to do it. Sometimes you just have to accept that some students have it in their minds that they are going to fail and you can't change their mind you can try and change their perception of themselves but they may have their own vision of their life and if they really perceive themselves as failing then that's what they are going to do, it doesn't mean they will fail forever.

[Questions from the Real World]

LouAnne Johnson

Question: At what point do we finally decide that enough is enough and realise we can't do everything for them?

LouAnne: Some adults take responsibility for the kids' behaviour, they teach the kids to be dependent. They are not babies, we have to hold them responsible for their behaviour – "you can make the choice to change your behaviour or you are going to have to leave the classroom, etc. etc."

I remember I had a kid who pulled my hair and when I asked him why he did it he said it was because he was B.D. I asked him what that meant and he said, "I am behaviour disordered" again I asked him what did that mean and he said, "Well I can't control my behaviour."

I said "I don't believe that - you've been in my classroom for a month and you controlled your behaviour every day until now."

I gave him the option to lie down on the floor, stand in the back of the room, step outside, whatever he needed to do to learn to control himself and said, "I don't care if you have been whatever for the past 10 or 12 years, you don't have to accept the label. Our brains are not carved in stone, you may test poorly at some time but that doesn't mean to say that you haven't learned something so let's deal with the present and not the past." – that's really important.

Mobile Phones

Policies regarding mobile phones vary from setting to setting so the way you address this problem will depend on the school/college's overall viewpoint. If the establishment you're working in has a definite rule and consequences in place regarding use of phones you can treat this as any usual behaviour problem and consistently stick to the policy. This can be such a huge problem, with students being so passionate about their phones, that enforcing the rules can be difficult. Here are four strategies you could consider:

1. Pre-empt and negate the need to take emergency calls. Students will always give the excuse that they need to be able to receive emergency calls from home on their phones. Maybe they do, maybe they don't but by sending a card home with the school/college number on and the assurance that any message will be passed on to the student immediately, you remove any need to have a phone.

2. Offer texting time. This can only be used where the setting has no clear procedure regarding the use of phones. If clear rules are in place you obviously can't be seen to openly abuse them; however if the issue is left up to you to sort out in your own way, you could consider offering students a few minutes at the end or middle of the lesson as a spontaneous reward for completing a task.

3. Use peer pressure. Set up an agreement with students whereby they can have an early finish/extra break time/computer access/video show etc in return for losing five minutes of this preferred activity time every time a phone is heard/seen/used in class. Anyone violating the rule will make themselves very unpopular.

4. Encourage use of phones as learning tools. Mobile phones now have hundreds of applications which can be effectively used to enhance education. While most public schools don't allow the devices because they're considered distractions, some schools and teachers have started to put the technology to positive use and this (quite surprisingly) seems to have led to a decline in inappropriate 'phone use during lessons.

At the most basic level a mobile phone can provide a basic suite of useful classroom tools. A class full of mobile phones means there is a full set of calculators and stopwatches right there that are able to be used without need for explanation, and without much risk of any being stolen or lost.

Most phones have cameras and while in the past students always had to draw diagrams to show their scientific method and to record evidence, now they can take a picture instead. It gives them something that they can put straight into a report.

Text messaging provides a means of communication which is a) immediate, b) easy to use and c) preferred by students. Sending regular reminders to students by text message (SMS) will be better received and less likely to be viewed as 'nagging' than face to face instruction; some students prefer to communicate through text rather than face to face contact. If it will help engage a difficult student or encourage a shy one to participate, why not utilise the technology?

Quick ideas for using mobile phones in school:

- Timing experiments with stopwatch

- Photographing apparatus and results of experiments for reports

- Photographing development of design models for e-portfolios

- Photographing texts/whiteboards for future review

- Bluetoothing project material between group members

- Receiving SMS & email reminders from teachers

- Recording a teacher reading a poem for revision

- Creating short narrative films using video

- Downloading, listening to and translating foreign language podcasts

- Answering questions delivered via podcasts

- Using GPS to identify locations

- Transferring files between school and home

- Translate information into 'text speak' (or have students translate information into Text Language as part of a review exercise)

- Use text to pass on information for discussion

- Use text to answer questions in a quiz – text the answer to an email or phone

- Send random questions to class members

- As an end-of-lesson review activity – students record by voice or text the key points learned and then save them in a suitable folder on their phones or text them to each other

- Planning world domination (iPhone apps available for this one)

The Class From Hell

You might recognise this class. It's composed largely of the 'known' offenders around the school. They won't listen to anything you say, they snub you or laugh in your face, they do little/no work, they talk over you and complain about every aspect of the lesson and life in general.

If you are fortunate enough to have been assigned one or more of these groups you will have no no-doubt tried everything to gain control. You've tried the 'shouty' method – and found it doesn't work. You've tried the non-shouting, 'friendly' method – and you've found that doesn't work either – you just got walked on. You've tried sending uncontrollable students out of the room but it's pretty much the entire class that's out of control and you can't get rid of all of them. Besides, most of these students get kicked out of lessons in other subjects and are on all kinds of whole school reports already - they don't care. So what can you do?

The first thing to understand is that this group has become accustomed to walking all over you and they are finding it quite rewarding. So, on a very basic level, we just need to make it MORE rewarding for them to behave appropriately and LESS rewarding for them to continue behaving as they are currently.

I find it helpful to remember that deep down, most students – even the members of the Class From Hell – want to do well, they almost always want to succeed and it's actually quite rare to find a whole group of students hell-bent on failure. It may seem as though they are determined to ruin everything but it's quite likely that most of the individuals simply don't realize there's an alternative and that it will be okay, despite the current level of negative peer pressure, to start following the rules and taking part.

You see, when they're caught up in a negative cycle it's very difficult for them to take positive action without some form of intervention. So it's very much up to us to provide the stimulation and direction they need to make necessary changes and then to provide the acknowledgement and support they need to encourage them to stick in and maintain their efforts.

To do this, we focus on positive reinforcement and on acknowledgement of any small steps they take in the right direction. We take time to build positive, trusting, respectful relationships with these students and show them that we value them and are there to support them. We give the ring-leaders responsibilities to show how much we trust them and value their input and skills. We take the time to contact parents regularly – keeping them notified of progress and building relationships with them so that they become our allies when we need some extra support. We show that our intention is for these students to succeed – we set work at an achievable level, we mark work promptly, teach concepts clearly and create a supportive environment in which 'trying' and 'working' is 'OK'. We focus on the behaviours we WANT to see – reminding, encouraging and acknowledging along the way – rather than scolding, complaining and nagging about those we DON'T want to see.

And we plan ahead; we make sure that we have equipment ready and working, we have 'emergency activities' on standby and we have a

'Divide and Conquer' seating plan in place which splits up the 'Likely Lads & Lasses'. We pre-empt problems by speaking to some students prior to the lesson - giving them additional support and encouragement before anything goes wrong. We have stepped consequences and scripts in place which we can calmly turn to should anyone veer off the tracks and we are fully aware of (and therefore able to avoid) situations and occurrences which would result in disruption and confrontation.

And then when things go wrong, which they invariably do in all classrooms from time to time, we address rule breakers firmly and calmly – without getting drawn into secondary behaviours, arguments and discussions. Whenever possible, we do this on a 1:1 basis - thus removing the pressures and problems associated with an audience. We operate on a 100% consistent basis, upholding our expectations and classroom rules and following-through on all warnings... every time... issuing stepped consequences.

If necessary, we remove (or get assistance to do so) out-of-control students from the classroom, but we PREPARE for such measures in advance; we approach colleagues in neighbouring classrooms to let us 'park' students should we get to this stage and we have 'fool-proof' work ready, with complete instructions for the student to complete with minimal fuss.

We keep records – records of progress made so that we can remind students, parents and other members of staff how well they are doing – and records of all incidents (who said/did what, and when they did so) so that we can contribute to meetings with parents, senior staff and outside agencies with total professionalism and from a position of authority. It is far better to be able to give a documented history of events which state exactly what happened, what was said and the time and date this all happened than to say something like "Well, erm, yes, Jonnie causes a lot of problems in lessons".

In short, we build ourselves a reputation as a consistent, firm, fair and approachable member of staff who is there to help these young people succeed and make the best of themselves. And it's amazing how quickly the Class From Hell changes when we change.

Quick Strategies

Students arriving late:

Here are some strategies to deal with students who are late...

- Have lesson objectives clearly displayed and easily accessible materials for collection by the student with minimum disruption

- Have a vacant seat available for late-comers

- Establish and teach a routine for late arrivals

- Focus on what is being done RIGHT - Have a reward system which recognises and rewards punctuality

- Be sensitive to individual pupil needs, worries and concerns – offer time for student to explain situation after the lesson

- Put support strategies in place if necessary

- Always follow up lateness and ensure student makes up missed work

- Keep records. Get student to fill in a form giving reason for late arrival and the time they arrived. Send copies home with notification of consequences if it continues.

Students not participating in lesson tasks:

Here are some strategies to deal with students who won't take part in lesson activities...

- Have a bank of topic-related work that can be completed independently, providing some challenge but requiring minimal support

- Offer support/set up support systems so that student can get assistance appropriately when needed

- Be quick to acknowledge all efforts to participate & mark work promptly with positive feedback

- Set up 1:1 session to ask student how you can help them to participate more.

Students not participating in group work:

Here are some strategies to deal with students who won't take part in cooperative group work sessions...

- Have an allocated area where a student who can't 'cope with' or chooses not join in the group work can be directed to sit and work in isolation

- Have spare materials to enable the student to continue the group work independently

- Organise the lesson into chunks to provide a way back into group work for the student who has opted out

- Clearly demonstrate & explain behaviour and social skills needed for group work

- Have visual reminders on display

Attention Seeking Behaviour:

Here are some strategies to deal with students who display attention-seeking behaviour...

- Tactical ignoring (balanced out with lots of proximity praise)

- Get up close – move into their space and run the lesson from this position for a while

- Remain very calm and avoid getting wound up and thus rewarding the behaviour with negative attention

- Agree non-verbal cues in advance with known trouble-makers

Swearing/Verbal Abuse:

Here are some strategies to deal with students who are rude & use offensive language...

- Have rules and routines in place and remind them of the consequences for bad language.

- Consistent approach – ALL incidents of bad language need to be followed up so as not to allow excuses for 'accidental' swearing.

- Tape record outbursts of foul language and explain that it can be played back to parents.

- Take out a note pad and say "I'm now recording what you're saying."

- Have a meeting with the pupil/s involved and ask them to suggest alternative ways of expressing/dealing with anger or alternative words to use when they are angry.

Not settling at the start of lessons:

Here are some strategies to deal with students who won't settle at the start of lessons...

- Allow some cooling off time of a few minutes after transitions and breaks to allow them to settle.

- Use the countdown technique with lots of proximity praise... "5; OK it's time to stop and look this way. Excellent, very quick on that table. 4; pens should be down, books and mouths should be closed, very good you two, you're listening to me. 3; still too much noise over here, that side of the room are perfect. 2; Just waiting for the last few people now, all conversations should be stopped, hands on the desk in front of you. Well done, you've got it. 1; Thank you."

- Have a visual reminder of noise levels such as coloured cards/traffic lights. When green is up the noise level in the room is fine. Orange – warning, level is too high and needs to drop immediately. If it doesn't drop after an agreed time, red card goes up. Red. Stop the activity, take a minute off break and insist on silent working for 5 minutes.

- Take control at the door – don't let them in the room until they're quiet.

Confrontation:

Here are some strategies to deal with students who are confrontational and argumentative...

- Adopt non-threatening body language (body to side, open arms)
- Avoid threatening hand gestures (pointing), facial expressions and verbal language (shouting, accusing)
- Diffuse and de-escalate – use humour, change subject.
- Calmly offer support...

"How can I help?" "I'm here to help. You tell me what's wrong, I'll just listen."

Disruption:

Here are some strategies to deal with students who are disruptive...

- Remove the audience factor, try and talk to them quietly on a 1:1 basis where possible and remind them of past successes and capabilities – try to find something positive to say first
- Give them a responsibility
- Use the 'language of choice':

"Do you want to move closer to the board or remain where you are?"

"Do you need me to help you or can you get on with things on your own?"

"What are you supposed to be doing? What happens if you don't do it? Is that what you want? What are you going to choose?"

- Calmly warn them of consequences and follow up...

"Jordan sit back down on your chair and finish the work please"

"Jordan, I'm asking you for the second and final time to sit down and get on with your work."

"Jordan you've chosen to ignore me. Go to Time Out."

Ignoring You:

Here are some strategies to deal with students who ignore you when you speak to them...

• Give very clear instructions so there is no room for confusion or argument.

• Try using humor to change their state from being angry or sullen.

• On a 1:1 basis with a pupil you normally get on well with try to find what is bothering them by calmly repeating statements such as:

"Tell me what's wrong so I can help you."

"You talk, I'll listen. Tell me what's bothering you, I'll just listen."

• Refuse to get drawn into confrontation –

"I've told you what you need to do and you know what happens if you don't. It's your choice, I'll be available after school if you want to discuss it then."

Lack of Equipment:

Here are some strategies to deal with students who 'forget' to bring equipment to class...

• Offer to loan them some of your equipment in return for 'collateral' such as a shoe

• Give a brief period of time at the start of the lesson for pupils to borrow items from other members of the class

• Reward those who bring required equipment

• Focus on teaching right action and correcting behaviour of persistent offenders: Offer them support in the way of special reminders and inform parents that this key issue is causing concern; get them to follow up at home and issue reminders at home.

Lack of Motivation:

Here are some strategies to deal with students who lack motivation...

• Set short term mini-targets:

"By the end of the lesson you need to get down to here in your text book."

"In the next ten minutes you need to complete numbers 1-4. I'll be back to check in ten minutes."

• Make lesson activities more active

• Include fun starters, video clips, educational games, energizers, magic tricks and brain teasers in your lessons from time to time to break up monotony

• Use loads and loads of effective praise and encouragement.

Off-Task (low level disruption):

Here are some strategies to deal with low-level disruption and off-task behaviours...

• Use pre-agreed non-verbal signals.

• Get close up – sit or stand close to them and say nothing, carry on with the lesson

• Use proximity and personal praise – Look for opportunities to catch them being good

• Look for opportunities to offer help... Offer choices, adjust the work, adjust seating

Defiance:

Here are some strategies to deal with defiant students...

- Offer support – often pupils are defiant because they are afraid of failure – adjust the work, offer help, ask them what's bothering them.

- Remind them of past successes and capabilities.

- Remind them that you are there to help them and ask them for help in how to bring that about.

"I need your advice. I want to help you – what is going to make this easier for you?"

- Go through stepped sanctions as per school behaviour policy...

➡ Give them a warning (verbal/name on board etc.) and remind them of consequences.

➡ Move them to an isolated seat.

➡ Take time off them at break/after school.

➡ Notify them of a letter/phone call home.

➡ Park them in another class.

Shouting Out:

Here are some strategies to deal with students who shout out in class...

- Ignore those who shout out and reward/praise those that ask questions appropriately

- Play class team games/quizzes where answers will only be accepted by those who put their hands up. Penalize team-members who shout out by taking a point off the team. (Teaching class rules in this way is far more effective than nagging).

- Have a clear policy on how questions are to be answered in class

- Keep those who shout in at break and explain that shouting won't be tolerated

Flatulence:

Here are some strategies to deal with students who use flatulence to disrupt lessons...

- Ignore it. By reacting you give them exactly what they were trying to elicit.

- Explain that if they do it again they will have to stay in at break for a lesson on healthy diet and the effect certain foods have on digestion

- Show great concern for their health and tell them it might be a good idea if you were to talk to their parents about it immediately by telephone if they are having trouble controlling it

- Follow normal procedure for disruptive behaviour but be careful not to appear confrontational or you will get the classic response "That's not fair, I can't help it."

Failing to Follow Instructions:

Here are some strategies to deal with students who won't follow instructions...

- Explain very clearly the consequence for not following instructions. Tell them you expect immediate compliance and then give them a few moments to save face by walking away.

- Record the details of the incident and follow up with senior staff.

- Warn them that you will be contacting parents and make sure you do so if the defiance continues

- Have the student removed from the classroom

- Start afresh next lesson – don't hold grudges.

Dealing with Crises, Conflict & Serious Incidents

The following steps are a progressive approach to dealing with major disruptions and crises.

Whatever you feel constitutes a crisis – be it a fight between students, or a whole class riot, the fact is that such events don't just happen out of the blue without build-up or warning.

A crisis situation doesn't just happen without build-up or warning.

There is always a trigger.

It is up to us to recognize these triggers, remove or reduce them where possible and respond early enough to prevent a problem getting out of control.

There are 2 clear stages leading up to a crisis or major outburst and our job is to try and prevent the event escalating from one stage to the next. The key to remember here is that if we allow a preceding stage to go unchecked, we are allowing the possibility for extreme and often quite frightening incidents to happen.

If you try to sort out a crisis once it is fully underway, you have far less chance of calming it down than you would of if you'd responded earlier to the warning signs.

The 2 stages leading up to a crisis

Stage 1: Response to a trigger

What to look for ...

Trigger experiences often don't happen when you're actually present. It may be that a child was upset by something that happened last night at home, it may have happened on the bus, it may have happened during break time or it may be an on-going bullying issue.

But, while we may not see the trigger event actually happen; the after-effects will be apparent in the student's mood and actions. As people become angry or anxious they give clear signals and it is in recognizing these signs of discomfort that enable us to prevent discomfort from bubbling into rage. Vigilance is the key!

Restlessness and fidgeting for example are sure signs of distress and anxiety, and should not be misconstrued as mere boredom or lack of application.

When a child who is normally placid becomes more agitated, it's easy to see that something's wrong; but equally telling might be a person who is normally animated becoming atypically passive and withdrawn.

If you know your students well enough (that's why positive teacher-student relationships are so important) they may show other signs that you have come to recognize as a sign that something is wrong; such as not answering you when you greet them.

Typical signs that a child may be experiencing distress include:

- Agitated behaviour such as pacing

- Refusal to take outdoor jacket/coat off

- Rigid body and crossed arms

- Repeated phrases

- Withdrawn, sulky and non-compliant

- Posturing – jutting jaw and/or chest stuck out

All these are signs that a child is distressed, angry or worried about something and unless you do something about it, that situation will only get worse.

Dealing with students in stage 1

Diversion and diffusion tactics are particularly useful – so be ready with changes of activity or anything that can engage them and take their mind away from whatever is causing distress.

It may a good idea to send the child on an errand in some circumstances to give them an escape route from circumstances that they're finding difficult without losing face ...

"David, could you go to the office and ask them for some board pens for me, please?"

Humour, as I've already mentioned, can be a terrific diffuser at stressful times and teachers who can react to threats in a light-hearted manner tend to quickly regain control. For example, responding to a child who has raised a chair to throw at someone else with something like ...

"Put my favourite chair down please – it can't stand heights" or

"Right, weapons down, books out"

... may be all that's needed to take the sting out of a fraught situation.

The aim of using humour in these circumstances is to change the internal state of the person as soon as possible – once you've broken their aggressive or anxious state, you can then work quietly with them to find out what was wrong and address the problem so it doesn't flare up again.

What to say to a child in Stage 1

Only by finding out what is causing a child distress can we actually do anything about it and the following script has proved an excellent, non-invasive form of questioning to reach that goal.

When students are wound up, they find it very difficult to convey their feelings through words, so their behaviour is actually a very definite cry for help. To calmly explain what it is that's bothering them is beyond the average angry teenager, and nagging them or pestering them for answers and reasons for their anger will often make matters worse.

The following script has proved very effective in getting even the most distressed students to 'open up' and explain the reasons for their irritation – without arousing further anger or distress. From here, we can then address the practical matters to help that child.

The magic script to use when you need to find out what is bothering a child

There are times when we need to find out what is bothering a child because it is interfering with their learning and/or disrupting the progress of your lesson and it is amazing just how effective the following script is for achieving that aim. I've seen some very distressed students who are refusing to speak to anyone, respond magically to this.

Remember, at the bottom of their hearts they want to be heard, they want to tell you what's on their mind, they want your attention and they want your help. Their problem is that they just don't possess the social skills to be able to voluntarily offload to you and they will only do so when they feel secure and are approached in the correct manner.

This short script shows students that you are aware they are bothered about something and through focused repetition shows that your sole intention is to help them.

It gives them the attention they need and helps them offload because there is no blame attached. You tell them very clearly and simply that you are only there to listen to them – not to judge them. It offers them the chance to have someone hear their whole story without being criticized.

Obviously, this script can only be used if you have a positive teacher-student relationship with the child you're trying to help; after-all, a child will only want to talk with someone they feel at ease with.

In order for it to work you first need to put some distance between the student and the rest of the class – it's unlikely they'll tell you what's wrong if their classmates are listening, especially if it involves them 'grassing' on another student.

"David ..."

(Use the student's name to gain their attention)

"David ... I can see that something is wrong"

(This acknowledges there is a problem and that you are aware of it without actually blaming them for something).

"Talk to me, tell me what's wrong and I'll listen."

"Tell me what's wrong and I may be able to help."

"Talk to me and I'll try and help."

"Talk to me, I'll listen."

In each case our words are clear and simple so as not to be misunderstood and are without blame or threat of consequence so as not to provoke an argument. The message is clear – we are simply there for them to talk to, to give their side of the story.

The trick with this script is that it must be repeated, repeated, repeated. As many times as is necessary until the child eventually tells you what is wrong.

And that's all there is to it. It may be simple, but it works...like magic.

Stage 2: Heightened distress and anxiety

What to look for...

• Verbal abuse, targeted offensive language, shouting.

• Aggressive body language such as clenched fists.

• Low level destruction of resources and property.

• Maybe becoming increasingly withdrawn and refusing to speak; younger children may hide under tables.

Dealing with students in stage 2

Diversion tactics may still work at this stage but it is likely that the behaviour will continue to get worse without additional support in the form of clear reminders of limits, boundaries, choices and consequences.

The aim must be to take the pressure out of the situation – not to add to it, even though it is very easy to lose your temper at this stage - so it is imperative that you remain calm and try to reduce the anxiety of the student. By becoming argumentative or overly authoritarian you risk becoming the target and making the situation worse.

Instructions should be given in a calm but firm manner.

What to say to a child in stage 2

When a child is in a heightened state of anxiety care has to be taken not to nag or say anything that will wind them up further. Getting drawn into a discussion or an argument must also be avoided because you will quickly become the target of their attack and render yourself unable to calm them down.

The best things to say at this stage are very simple instructions together with reminders that you are there to help them. One way of doing this is to offer them a set of clear, limited choices.

Being given a choice when you're wound up is a tremendous relief whereas being given orders or told you can't do this and that is very frustrating and simply fuels the feeling of anxiety and anger.

"Paul, I want to help you calm down so that you don't end up in trouble. I have two choices for you to help you. You can come and sit at the front away from everyone else until you feel better or you can take 2 minutes outside the door if it will help. Which do you want to do?"

You can also use **the 3 requests technique** (Next chapter, tool #2) as this is a perfect method of reminding a student how far they have pushed things and what the consequences will be. It also helps you keep calm. The only thing I would say is that you have to be very careful about the way you phrase it. You must convey total detachment and refrain from being cynical, aggressive or provocative.

At this stage it may be necessary to remove the child from the classroom or activity area for reasons of safety and you should be very clear about your school's policy regarding this.

Additional Tools

1. The five-step script to get students back on task:

i) State what you want them to do calmly and clearly.

The first thing to do is state very clearly what they are doing wrong and what they have to do to put it right. You need to make their choices as simple as possible and leave no room for misunderstanding. As usual there's no need to get annoyed or raise your voice to show you're in charge – just calmly make the statement in short, clear sentences. You also need to explain why they should do what you're asking – i.e. tell them what will happen once they've followed your instructions. By doing this you show that you're not just getting on their backs for the sake of it. This of course, gives them fewer reasons to complain or argue against your instructions.

"John you're not doing your work and other people are being distracted by you. You need to pick your pen up and finish your target so that you don't have to get it finished in your own time."

Finally notice how the requests are phrased in a positive, not negative way. For example "Stop wandering" or "Stop talking" are both negative commands.

If they don't immediately start doing as you've asked or if they answer you with a promise to do it soon, you should move on to stage 2.

(A promise that they will do as you ask "in a minute" or "later" is their way of controlling the situation – treat it as if they have ignored you).

ii) Explain exactly what will happen to them if they continue to misbehave.

Tell them very clearly what the sanction will be if they continue to defy you. Use a matter-of-fact tone. Remember not to get angry or raise your voice – you don't want to reward this behaviour with emotion - you need to convey total and utter control. For that reason, once you get to this stage, even if you normally have a 'friendly' approach, there is no longer a place for humour.

Also, under no circumstances should you get drawn in to an argument as this gives the impression that you haven't fully made up your mind. If the student manages to draw you into a discussion of any kind they will think there must be a chance you'll change your mind. Once they see an opening, they will try to exploit it with more and more arguing.

"If you don't manage to get the work that I've set for you finished, you will end up losing 5 minutes of break."

"If you don't stop throwing the bits of eraser you'll have to spend your break clearing the floor."

iii) Now you need to give them time to carry out your instruction. Immediately follow on by giving them a time limit and then back off to give them some space.

"I'll be back in about 30 seconds – when I come back you need to have done as I've asked."

With a clear choice spelled out to them like this you'll be surprised how easy it is for them to do the right thing. Once they have had it clearly spelled out to them exactly where the boundary is and that continuing their misbehaviour will result in a specific sanction, they soon change. By clearly explaining exactly what they are doing wrong, exactly what they must do to put it right and exactly what will happen if they continue the behaviour, you are also being completely fair. You are still maintaining total control but by giving them a clear, limited choice you make it easy for them to do the right thing.

And by backing off – walking to another part of the room or going to help another student, you're giving them a chance to back down without losing face; you're giving them an escape route. When a child has backed themselves into a corner it's difficult for them to back down in front of their classmates if you're standing over them. If you say your piece and then stand there staring at them they will become intimidated in front of their friends and react accordingly – usually with more defiance. By walking away you take pressure off them so there is more chance of them doing the right thing.

iv) If they do as you've asked, acknowledge it!

It's a big step they've just taken. Don't lecture them about how they should follow instructions faster next time - just give them a sincere smile and some quiet private praise.

"I'm impressed John – well done."

That's all that's needed to let them know they did the right thing and to encourage them to do it in future. With younger students the compliance can be rewarded more formally – perhaps by getting them to place a sticker on a chart for meeting the behaviour target "Follow teacher's instructions".

What if they don't do as you've asked?

If they won't comply then you can simply state the sanction or consequence that they must now face:

"Ok you've chosen to carry on doing...... That's fine. You'll be staying in at break for 5 minutes. Now get on with your work so that you don't lose any more of your time."

Once again, give them a few moments to think and settle.

What's of paramount importance is that you follow up on your consequence. This will have a very positive effect on the other lively members of your group because it shows you have total control but also that you are totally fair. It's important for other children in the group to witness that.

v) If the consequence has little or no effect…

If the student resumes the behaviour, repeat the procedure with a tougher consequence. This is why you should always start off with a small consequence so that you can increase it if necessary.

2. The 3 Requests Technique that helps you keep calm and gives you instant control

Would you like to know how to keep your temper when dealing with the most demanding students? Wouldn't it be amazing to be able to remain calm in even the most frustrating, anxiety-ridden situations – to never shout, or display a lack of control of any kind?

How would it feel to be able to say a couple of sentences to a child and have them immediately do as you ask? No more battle of wills, no more confrontation. It would be like suddenly gaining 50 years of experience in one fell swoop; like becoming a Zen master of behaviour management overnight.

The 3 Requests Technique is a stepped response that leads to a known punishment such a time out, phone call home, detention etc. and can dramatically reduce pressure in any confrontational situation. The beauty of this is that the child knows exactly where they are in terms of boundaries.

The three Requests technique gives you total control in any confrontational situation. It prevents irritation and frustration escalating to rage, as is often the case when students refuse to follow our instructions. And it also prevents us, as staff, from issuing sanctions and punishments which the students would consider unfair.

Indeed, the success of this method lies in its fairness on the student. It gives them a very clear warning that their behaviour is unacceptable, and gives them the opportunity to address it.

They know, because of the very clear, succinct instructions, exactly what will happen to them next. It gives them a clear warning that their behaviour will definitely result in the known sanction if they continue.

Students become enraged if they are given a sanction with no apparent warning but this technique gives them a clear choice of whether to accept the consequence of their action or change their behaviour to avoid it.

Finally it gives them a definite deadline by which to make that choice. Add to this the fact that it is totally non-confrontational and in my opinion, you have the perfect strategy for gaining compliance from disobedient children.

How to use the 3 requests technique

Basically it's an almost fool-proof, non-confrontational way of getting your instructions followed but the best way of explaining it is by way of an example ...

Let's consider the following response to a student who keeps getting out of his chair and walking round the room...

The teacher, on recognizing that Joe is agitated about something first tries offering more support – she asks him if anything's wrong or offers him more help with the work . She gives him a work target, offers him a different seat, tries humour etc. etc. but Joe continues to get out of his chair and bother other students.

The teacher says (in a very calm tone) ...

"Joe, you're out of your chair. Please return to your seat and get on with your work."

[Pause]

"If you want to get in the lunch queue on time with everyone else you need to go back to your seat now - otherwise I'll have to keep you back for five minutes after the lesson."

The teacher turns away for a few moments to look at another student's work and give Joe time to concede defeat without looking a fool.

Joe continues to walk round the room.

At this point the teacher moves within close proximity of the child and repeats her instruction in a calm, non-confrontational manner...

"Joe, I'm asking you for the second time to return to your seat."

At this stage it is crucial to maintain a calm voice – the teacher doesn't need to raise her voice or get angry – she just lets the script do the work.

If Joe complied at this point the teacher would reinforce the fact that he had followed instructions by immediately verbally rewarding his appropriate behaviour.

She wouldn't berate him for not following instructions earlier and she wouldn't ignore his compliance. She would acknowledge it and immediately reward it before moving on with the lesson. Why? Because she wants him to follow her instructions next lesson too - and the best way to make this happen is by convincing him that doing so is a rewarding experience for him.

If Joe still didn't do as he was asked at this stage the teacher would ensure she had his attention and the instructions would be repeated one last time...

"Joe this is the third and final time I'm going to ask you to sit down and get on with your work."

It is important that the instruction is brief and direct, but again, that the voice isn't raised or accompanied by an emotional reaction of any sort. The teacher remains calm and lets the script do the work. She doesn't get drawn into debates, arguments or explanations. The child knows exactly what he has to do to avoid a consequence; there is no need to provide any further reasoning.

If Joe finally managed to follow the request, he would be praised as above.

If he still persisted in behaving inappropriately he would then be notified of the sanction.

"Joe you were asked 3 times to sit down. You haven't done as I said. Go to time out."

"Joe you haven't followed instructions. You must go to see Mr. Blakey."

"Joe you haven't followed instructions. You've got yourself a detention."

Following the sanction the teacher must then be vigilant for any demonstration of positive behaviour by the child which she can then praise.

Always the approach must be to give attention to the right behaviour whenever possible.

If the child still refuses to follow instructions and return to work after the sanction has been given or if the behaviour escalates then further management is clearly required.

If the student remains calm but defiant then the strategy would be to return to the early stages of the stepped approach – concentrating on giving support to the student, talking with them, perhaps withdrawing them to a quiet area for a while to try and find out the reason for the behaviour.

If the student starts to get angry and becomes verbally or physically abusive then we would need to adopt strategies from Part 3.

3. Ten Magic words to make a disruptive child behave

I have found an excellent phrase for making children really think about their behaviour and enabling them to choose more sensible alternatives. I add this phrase once I've explained what the consequence will be.

"Is that what you want to happen? It's your choice"

So our new statement would be ...

"If you don't manage to get the work that I've set for you finished, you will end up losing 5 minutes of break. Is that what you want to happen? It's your choice."

By adding this phrase your doing two very important things here – making them really think about where their behaviour is leading them – "is that what you want to happen?" and then reminding them that the way out is completely within their control – that they have a clear choice – "It's your choice."

In effect this helps them out of the hole they've dug for themselves – it gives them a ladder - and it helps them take responsibility for their behaviour.

4. How to say 'no' to a student without causing an argument

When a student makes an unreasonable demand it's difficult to know what to say. Some children – particularly those with limited social skills and behavioural difficulties find it very difficult to accept a categorical "No".

One way round this is to say 'yes' instead – but to also add a condition. I call this the 'Conditional Yes'.

"Sir, can we do a poster this lesson?"

"NO."

"Why not? We did one last lesson! I'm doing a poster!"

And on and on and on.

The conditional yes is an answer to their question consisting of three parts:

1. "That sounds great."

2. "The only drawback is…"

3. "So how about this as an alternative …?"

"Sir, can we do a poster?"

"Hey what a good idea Brian – especially after the fantastic job you made of the last ones." (That sounds great.)

"The thing is, we've got to get this English task done as part of your coursework." (The only drawback is …)

"How about you illustrate your coursework when you've finished?"

or

"Get your coursework finished and then you can do a poster about it."

(Here's an alternative ...)

It works almost every time as long as you're firm about the drawback and offer a reasonable alternative. Kids know the rules – they just like pushing them so we need to show that we will accommodate their desires (on our terms) whilst remaining in total control.

5. A simple sentence that reduces disruption by 50%

In their book, 'You Can ...You know you can.' (2001), Maines and Robinson found a 50% reduction in disruptive behaviours following the introduction of a structured script for teachers for use when giving directions.

They state that communication can be improved and a situation can be de-personalized when staff begin their instructions with "When you ... (state behaviour)" and ends with an explanation of the resulting effect "then I ... (state what the behaviour causes)."

For example, rather than saying "You need to stop interrupting" or "You're holding up the lesson", we would say ...

"Vicky, when you shout across the room it disturbs other people. Please get on with your work without shouting."

Or:

"Greg, when you interrupt me, it makes it difficult for people to hear and I can't teach the lesson properly. Please listen quietly".

Following a tight script like this makes you focus on what you're saying and you're then less likely to lose your temper.

And Finally!

"It made my naughtiest student as quiet as a mouse!"

"Thank you so much for the superbly wonderful videos! I benefited a lot from your creative secret agent method! It made my naughtiest student as quiet as a mouse! THANK YOU..."

Yasaman Shafiee (Take Control of the Noisy Class customer)

Take Control of The Noisy Class

To get your copy, go here:

https://www.amazon.co.uk/Take-Control-Noisy-Class-Super-effective/dp/1785830082/

Also, if you'd like to receive my FREE **Behaviour Tips** on an inconsistent and irregular basis via my email service, just sign up for your FREE Classroom Management Mini-Course and you'll start receiving my Behaviour Tips.

Sign up for your FREE copy here:

http://needsfocusedteaching.com/kindle/behaviour/

These contain short, practical ideas and strategies for responding to all kinds of inappropriate classroom behaviour, as well as some handy teaching tips and ideas for improving student engagement. All this will be sent direct to your email inbox once or twice a week, along with occasional notifications about some of our other products, special offers etc.

Obviously, you can opt out of this service any time you wish but in our experience, most people pick up a lot of *wonderful* ideas from these emails. And feel free to forward the messages and resources on to other teachers (staff meetings, staff room, pop them into your Christmas cards etc.).

Just remember to look out for emails from '***Needs Focused Teaching***' so that you don't miss all the goodies.

"Thanks a million. As a fresh teacher, I find this invaluable."

"Finally something concrete and applicable in real life – I've had enough of the people who have never set their foot in a real classroom but know how everything should be done in theory. Thanks a million. As a fresh teacher, I find this invaluable."

Jasna (Take Control of the Noisy Class customer)

Review Request

If you enjoyed this book, please leave me an honest review! Your support really does matter and it really does make a difference. I do read all the reviews so I can get your feedback and I do make changes as a result of that feedback.

If you'd like to leave a review, then all you need to do is go to the review section on the book's Amazon page. You'll see a big button that states "Write a customer review". Click on that and you're good to go!

You can also use the following links to locate the book on Amazon:

https://www.amazon.com/dp/B0754NNJ7S

https://www.amazon.co.uk/dp/B0754NNJ7S

For all other countries, please head over to the relevant Amazon site and either search for the book title or simply copy and paste the following code in the Amazon search bar to be taken directly to the book:

B0754NNJ7S

Have fun and thanks for your support...

Rob

"...your strategies work wonders!"

"Thank you so much Rob for what you are doing for the profession, your strategies work wonders! I have never tried the 'pen' but will do next time! Seriously speaking, I give the link to your productions to many young teachers I know because they are so unhappy sometimes and they need help which they find with what you do! So, thanks again and carry on with your good job!"

Marie (Take Control of the Noisy Class customer)

Suggested resource providers

Name: HowtoLearn.com and HowtoLearn.teachable.com

Specialty: Personalized Learning Assessments, Learning Solutions, Courses for Teachers, Parents and Students.

Website: www.HowtoLearn.com

Details: Online since 1996, the brainchild of best-selling author and college professor, Pat Wyman, known as America's Most Trusted Learning Expert. We invite you to become part of our global community and closed Facebook group. Your Learning Questions Answered at http://www.HowtoLearn.com/your-learning-questions-answered.

Resources: Take our Free Learning Styles Quiz at HowtoLearn.com and check out parent/teacher tested and approved courses at HowtoLearn.teachable.com.

* * *

Name: Time Savers for Teachers (Stevan Krajnjan)

Speciality: Resources guaranteed to save you time.

Website: http://www.timesaversforteachers.com/ashop/affiliate.php?id=7

Details: Popular forms, printable and interactive teacher resources that save time. Stevan Krajnjan was presented with an Exceptional Teacher Award by The Learning Disabilities Association of Mississauga and North Peel in recognition for outstanding work with children who have learning disabilities.

Resources: www.timesaversforteachers.com

* * *

Name: Nicola Morgan (NSM Training & Consultancy).

Speciality: Innovative resources to motivate staff and empower schools.

Website: www.nsmtc.co.uk

Details: NSM Training & Consultancy provides high quality training for teaching/non teaching staff in the UK and internationally. We provide a large range of courses, expert consultancy and guidance, publications, conferences as well as innovative resources to motivate staff and empower schools.

Resources: http://www.nsmtc.co.uk/resources/

* * *

Name: Susan Fitzell

Speciality: Special Education Needs

Website: www.SusanFitzell.com

Details: Seminar Handouts and supplemental resources for Differentiated Instruction, Motivation, Special Education Needs, Co-teaching, and more.

Resources: http://downloads.susanfitzell.com/

* * *

Name: Patricia Hensley

Speciality: Special Education

Website: http://successfulteaching.net

Details: Strategies and ideas for all grade levels. Great resource for new and struggling teachers.

Resources: Free Student Job Description. https://successfulteaching.blogspot.com/2007/10/student-job-description.html

* * *

Name: Julia G. Thompson

Speciality: Educational consultant, writer, and presenter.

Website: www.juliagthompson.com.

Details: Author of The First-Year Teacher's Survival Guide, Julia G Thompson specializes in assisting new teachers learn to thrive in their new profession.

Resources: For 57 free forms and templates to make your school year easier, just click go to her website and click on the Professional Binder page

* * *

Name: Steve Reifman

Speciality: Teaching the Whole Child (Empowering Classroom Management & Improving Student Learning)

Website: www.stevereifman.com

Details: National Board Certified Elementary Teacher & Amazon Best-Selling Author.

Author of '10 Steps to Empowering Classroom Management: Build a Productive, Cooperative Culture Without Using Rewards'

Resources: https://www.youtube.com/user/sreifman (FREE, 1-2 minute videos with tips for teachers & parents)

*　*　*

Name: Dave Vizard

Speciality: Behaviour Management

Website: www.behavioursolutions.com

Details: Creator of Brain Break materials and Ways to Manage Challenging Behaviour ebook.

Resources: www.behavioursolutions.myshopify.com/pages/brain-breaks

*　*　*

Name: Marjan Glavac

Specialty: Tips on getting a teaching job (resume, cover letter, interviews); classroom management strategies.

Website: www.thebusyeducator.com

Details: Marjan Glavac is a best selling motivational author, engaging speaker and elementary classroom teacher with over 29 years of teaching experience.

Resources: Free weekly newsletter, 4 free eBooks (http://thebusyeducator.com/homepage.htm)

* * *

Name: Dr. Rich Allen

Specialty: Workshops and keynotes on engagement strategies for students of all ages

Website: greenlighteducation.net

Details: Author of 'Green Light Teaching' and 'The Rock 'n Roll Classroom'

Resources: Please join our Teaching tips community and access lots of free resources and ideas for your classroom by clicking HERE.

* * *

Name: Ross Morrison McGill

Speciality: Managing director at TeacherToolkit Ltd.

Website: https://www.teachertoolkit.co.uk/

Details: Ross Morrison McGill is a deputy headteacher working in an inner-city school in North London. He is the Most Followed Teacher on Twitter in the UK and writes the Most Influential Blog on Education in the UK.

Resources: https://www.amazon.co.uk/Ross-Morrison-McGill/e/B00G33GTEO/ref=dp_byline_cont_book_1

What people say about us

"Even if you have never had "the class from hell", there is something here for you"

"As a PGCE student it is great to have the opportunity to pick up user-friendly and easily accessible information. The 'Behaviour Needs' course provides exactly that. In a series of amusing, creative, fast-paced sections, Rob Plevin builds up a staggering amount of practical and thought provoking material on classroom behaviour management. All of which are easily translated back in the classroom. Even if you have never had "the class from hell", there is something here for you and the follow up information from the website is laden with golden nuggets which will give you loads more ideas and interventions."

Steve Edwards (Workshop Attendee and Take Control of the Noisy Class customer)

* * *

"I want you to know that you have changed the lives of 40 of my students."

"What an informative day. The sessions on positive reinforcement and the importance of relationships were particularly memorable. I want you to know that you have changed the lives of 40 of my students. Thank you!"

Joanne W. (Singapore Workshop Attendee)

*   *   *

"...We will be inviting Rob back on every possible occasion to work with all of our participants and trainees."

"We were delighted to be able to get Rob Plevin in to work with our Teach First participants. From the start his dynamic approach captivated the group and they were enthralled throughout. Rob covered crucial issues relating to behaviour management thoroughly and worked wonders in addressing the participants' concerns about teaching in some of the most challenging schools in the country. We will be inviting Rob back on every possible occasion to work with all of our participants and trainees."

Terry Hudson, (Regional Director 'Teach First', Sheffield Hallam University)

*   *   *

"Thank you for helping me to be in more control."

"Rob, thank you very much for sharing your experience and reminding of these simple but effective things to do. Students' behaviour (or actually my inability to control it) is so frustrating that at times it feels that nothing can help. Thank you for helping me to be in more control."

Natasha Grydasova (Take Control of the Noisy Class customer)

* * *

"I am HAPPILY spending my Sat afternoon listening, watching and reading all your extremely helpful information!"

"Thank You Rob! What a wealth of excellent ideas! This is my 30th year teaching! You would think after 30 years teaching that I wouldn't need to be viewing your awesome videos and reading your helpful blog and website. However, I am HAPPILY spending my Sat afternoon listening, watching and reading all your extremely helpful information! Thank You So Much! I will be one of your biggest fans from now on!"

Kelly Turk (Needs Focused Video Pack customer)

* * *

"...terrific for those teachers who are frustrated."

"Great easy-to-listen-to video tips that will be terrific for those teachers who are frustrated.

I'm forwarding this email on to the principals in my district right away!"

Sumner price (Take Control of the Noisy Class customer)

*   *   *

"Many thanks for all these really helpful life-savers!"

"Very many thanks. I have given myself trouble by letting kids into the room in a restless state with inevitable waste of teaching time. Your advice on calming them down in a positive, non-confrontational way and building rapport is very timely. Many thanks for all these really helpful life-savers!"

Philip Rozario (Take Control of the Noisy Class customer)

*   *   *

"Fantastic way to create a calm and secure learning environment for all the students."

"Thanks so much Rob. Fantastic way to create a calm and secure learning environment for all the students. It's great how you model the way we should interact with the students – firmly but always with respect."

Marion (Take Control of the Noisy Class customer)

*   *   *

"I will be recommending that the teachers in training that I deal with should have a look at these videos."

These tips and hints are put in a really clear, accessible fashion. As coordinator of student teachers in my school, I will be recommending that the teachers in training that I deal with should have a look at these videos.

Deb (Take Control of the Noisy Class customer)

*   *   *

"I found Rob Plevin's workshop just in time to save me from giving up."

"I found Rob Plevin's workshop just in time to save me from giving up. It should be compulsory – everybody in teaching should attend a Needs-Focused workshop and meet the man with such a big heart who will make you see the important part you can play in the lives of your most difficult students."

Heather Beames (Workshop Attendee)

*　*　*

"...the ideas, strategies and routines shared with our teachers have led to improved classroom practice."

"The Needs Focused Behaviour Management workshops in support of teacher training in Northern Ireland have been very well received and the ideas, strategies and routines shared with our teachers have led to improved classroom practice. This has been validated by both inspections at the University and observations of teachers."

Celia O'Hagan, (PGCE Course Leader, School of Education, University of Ulster)

*　*　*

"I have never enjoyed a course, nor learnt as much as I did with Rob."

"What a wonderfully insightful, non-patronising, entertainingly informative day. I have never enjoyed a course, nor learnt as much as I did with Rob. I was so impressed that I am recommending our school invite Rob along to present to all the staff so that we can all benefit from his knowledge, experience and humour."

Richard Lawson-Ellis (Workshop Attendee)

* * *

"...since I started following the principles in your materials, I have seen a vast improvement."

"Hi Rob, I would just like to say that since I started following the principles in your materials, I have seen a vast improvement. I had to teach a one hour interview lesson yesterday and was told that they thought the lesson was super and they loved my enthusiasm! I got the job!

Diane Greene (_Take Control of the Noisy Class customer_)

* * *

"Thanks to you, students from 30 some schools are truly engaged and not throwing pencils at the sub!"

Rob, Your student engagement series has been out of this world. I've already used various techniques as a substitute and students said I was **the best sub ever.** Thanks to you, students from 30 some schools are truly engaged and not throwing pencils at the sub!"

Leslie Mueller (Student Engagement Formula customer)

* * *

"So often professional development training is a waste of time; you may get one little gem from a whole day of training. You've given numerous strategies in 5 minutes."

Wow! So many people have gained so much from your videos! Teachers are time poor. A quick grab of effective ideas is what we all need. So often professional development training is a waste of time; you may get one little gem from a whole day of training. You've given numerous strategies in 5 minutes. Thanks for your generosity.

Mary – Ann (Take Control of the Noisy Class customer)

Strategies List

Made in the USA
San Bernardino, CA
31 May 2019